Monkey in a Pink Canoe

by
Allen Smith

Monkey in a Pink Canoe

by

Allen Smith

Copyright © 2014

All rights reserved. No part of this book may be reproduced in any form by any electronic or mechanical means including photocopying, recording, or information storage and retrieval without permission in writing from the author.

Cover design by M.R. Paxson

Cover illustration by Julia Fryer

juliavhfryer.co.uk

ISBN-978-0-9895406-5-0

Author's Website: http://snowwriter.com/

Published by Relentlessly Creative Books

Publisher's Website: http://relentlesslycreativebooks.com/

773-831-4944

USA

Other titles by Allen Smith

Watching Grandma Circle the Drain

Ski Instructors Confidential:

The Stories Ski Instructors Swap Back at the Lodge

Monkey in a Pink Canoe

To my family

Table of Contents

The $84 Windpipe 9
Uniforms are Rank 15
I'll Never Forget the Time I Remembered 19
A Prescription for Struggle. 23
Bank Robbery Made Easy. 27
My Sizzling Russian Bride 31
Don Ho Versus the Norwegians 35
New Horizons in Weight Control 39
A Little Baggage Never Hurt Anyone 43
Better Living through Drug Addiction. 47
Alcohol Of Fame 51
Minutes from Lorraine 55
Dealin' Delbert's Fine Used Babies 59
Feng Shui-ing My Chakras. 63
Great Moments in Digital History. 69
Shenandoahs, Pixie Cuts & Afrobobs. 73

Bwuck-Bwuck-Bwuck, Phltttttt 77
Paws for Prisoners 81
Betty Crocker Means Good Nutrition 85
I Don't Feel as Good as I Look 89
Space-Aged, High-Capacity Sports Bras 93
The Benefits of Benefits 97
The Happiest Peak on Earth 101
Those Good Old Time Diseases 105
Last Chance Undies 109
The Mother of All Boredom 113
The Taco-Slinging Road-Kill Handler 117
Interview with a Felon 121
Hoarding is the Life for Me 125
With Rentals Like These, Who Needs Friends? 129
Wonder Butts and Instant Face Lifts 133
Stranded in Purgatory 139
Reincarnation Gone Cluck 143
Smoke 'em if Ya Got 'em 147
Happy Birthday to Me 151
Monkey in a Pink Canoe 155
The Games People Play 159
The Triple Nipple Club 163
Shake My Hand or I'll Kiss You 167
Become a Breast Surgeon—Online! 171
Employment is a Full-Time Job 175
The Boys of Summer 179
38 Million Minutes to Go 183
I Remember Hugh 187
You Can't Compete with a Serial Killer 191
After I'm Dead 195
About the Author 198
Relentlessly Creative Books 200

The $84 Windpipe

"Never eat at a restaurant where the waiters wear spoons around their necks."

That was the cost-conscious advice my rabbi proffered as I was trying to decide where to celebrate the first day of my girlfriend's Rumspringa. I met Abhilasha Maddox online through Hotamishsingles.com and wanted to mask my stinginess by treating her to an upscale dinner at Reynaldo's. My hope was that she would abandon her religious way of life to come live with me in the room I rented from my parents.

As it turns out, my rabbi wasn't referring to a waiter—the correct term is sommelier—and Reynaldo's was crawling with them. Plus, those weren't spoons around their necks—they were "tastevins" —shallow, engraved cups designed to help embrace the appearance, aroma, finish, complexity, character, romance, potential or faults of a wine when determining what pairs best with Beluga, agar-agar or chaudfroid. I had no idea that an alcoholic beverage could have character or romance. What I did know was this dinner was going to vaporize the down payment I'd saved for my house, so I'd better enjoy it.

The sommeliers notwithstanding, I began to suspect I was in trouble when the hostess asked, "Would you care to see the appetizer menu?" Gold embossed and bound in leather, they sat prominently displayed along the top of her station like a set of World Book Encyclopedias. Most eateries I frequent have the appetizers printed on paper placemats and usually include such delicacies as buffalo wings, fried mozzarella sticks, loaded potato skins and cheddar smothered nachos. All you can eat for $5.95.

I sensed I was in over my head as I scanned a series of unintelligible items followed by the weather on Maui—it had to be a temperature. It was too high to be a price:

Haggis canapé giardiniera on brioche toast—84.00

I had no idea what Haggis canapé giardiniera on brioche toast was, so I told Abhilasha Maddox that I was going to the restroom to wash my hands. Crouched inside a handicap stall, I Googled the expression on my iPhone and nearly gagged when I learned it was crushed sheep's windpipe, heart and lungs mixed with vegetables served on fancy dry bread. No wonder they hid the ingredients under a continental shroud. Who, in their right mind, would start off their evening by eating $84 worth of crushed windpipe?

This continued with Gorgonzola, Oysters Bienville, au fromage, caciocavallo cheese, beurre, foie gras and Plugrá butter. Sensing another impending panic attack, I snuck a Valium and pulled our waiter aside to translate the rest of the menu before we sat down. I slipped him a $20 bill and confessed that the only things I recognized were toast, fries and beans. We were seated before I had a chance to run.

We opted for a booth toward the back of the dining room. Twenty more bucks got us a table away from the kitchen doors but close enough to the rear exit to sprint for it if the bill got too high. Over the years, fleeing expensive restaurants has become a way of life for me—especially if they don't take Olive Garden gift cards.

Gaston, our waiter, seated us at a linen-covered table for two that was set with more china, cutlery and glassware than I'd seen at Crate 'N Barrel. Orbiting around my service plate was a salad fork, fish fork, dinner fork, dinner knife, fish knife, salad knife, spoon, oyster fork and five types of glassware: a water goblet, champagne flute, red wine glass, white wine glass and a cordial/ sherry glass. Our table had more glasses than a Lenscrafters.

Above my service plate was a dessert spoon, dessert fork and butter knife. Since neither of us drank alcohol, I knew that we wouldn't need four out of the five flutes and goblets. Maybe they'd give us a discount. But it also raised the question, does having a fish fork mean that you're required to order fish? What if you're not going to have a salad? Or oysters? Do they still charge you for all those unused utensils? It reminded me of the time I had my appendix out. The insurance adjuster showed me a copy of the bill from the surgeon and anesthesiologist. Apparently, they charged me for a bone chisel, Doyen intestinal forceps and dozens of other instruments that had nothing to do with my appendix, so I guessed it would be the same at Reynaldo's. I just wish I could have taken the oyster fork home. My mother has never seen one.

Gaston returned and officially welcomed us to Reynaldo's and reminded us that if we wanted to order the Limoncello Souffle, we should do so now; it takes 13 chefs and three days to make each one. Then, it was time for the specials.

"Tonight's specials include an extraordinary jamon iberico de belotta imported from the Albacete hinterlands of Spain," boasted Gaston. "As a special treat, we also have Wild Fijian sashimi on a bed of tendril salad, sprinkled with toasted Kurrajong and drizzled with melon cilantro vinaigrette." To offset the blank glaze that was slowly washing over my face, I ordered one of each. Abhilasha Maddox settled on the Parsnip Mousselin in Apricot Agri-doux with Ginger Infused Cobia Puree. Fortunately, it was in season or she might have had her entire evening ruined by having to settle for the Hommard a L'amoricaine in a demi-glace caponate suspended on maquechoux and flageolet beans.

After we placed our order, we were visited by the Executive Chef, the Sous Chef, the Chef d Partie, the Saucier, the Boulanger, Confiseur, Poissonier, Friturier, the Patissier, Potager, the Tournant, both valets, the entire kitchen staff, the maintenance man and the janitor. All welcomed us to Reynaldo's and hoped that our experience would be memorable while they held out their hands for a $20 tip.

It wasn't until dining at Reynaldo's that I learned the first of a series of valuable gastronomic theorems. The first was Archimedes' Law of Squared Parabolas. In layman's terms, there is an inverse relationship between the price of the entree and how much of it comes in physical contact with your plate. A Double Whopper Sandwich Meal and all its accouterments costs $3.49 and covers the entire table. Conversely, my Cuitlacoche in copha asafetida with accompanying haricot vert and thrice baked papillote potatoes was precariously balanced on an eight inch-high tower supported by three baby scallions, highlighted by six delicate miso smears along the left border of the plate. Three dots of puttanesca insured that the price competed with the Gross Domestic Product.

The second theorem I learned was Eratosthenes' Order of Polyhedrons. The theorem states that the total price of your dining experience is the price of the entrees, multiplied by the cost of your appetizer, divided by dessert. Halfway through my Liederkrantz and arugula salad, I estimated my portion alone, would be somewhere around $525.

As we were finishing our main courses, Gaston cleared the table, setting the scene for dessert. "Along with your Limoncello soufflé, may I suggest a light Whippleberry akutaq?" Akutaq is a nice way of describing Eskimo ice cream made from reindeer fat, seal oil, freshly fallen snow and a hint of ground fish. It's anyone's guess where Reynaldo's found freshly fallen snow in Los Angeles during the summer. Maybe they had it flown in from Sitka. The price certainly justified it.

Despite being stuffed to the gills, emotionally and financially bankrupt, Gaston still had room for one more jab. "May I offer you an after dinner beverage to cleanse your palate? We have an excellent variety of ratafias with morello cherry kernels, infused with spices from the Bhairahawa region of Nepal. Or, perhaps I could interest you in a Caramel Macchiato with freshly steamed milk and vanilla, hand-pollenated by the natives of Papua New Guinea."

What an asshole.

As I anticipated, the final bill dispelled any illusion of realizing the American Dream—at least in this lifetime. Tips for the valet sealed the deal. But, at least Abhilasha Maddox was impressed. I dropped her off at her aunt Stolzfus' where she was staying for the week. "How was dinner?" she asked. "What did you have?" For the life of me, I couldn't remember. I'd spent the entire evening anguishing over the cost of our crushed windpipe, reindeer fat, seaweed and diseased duck liver. I'll have to go back and order it again.

Uniforms are Rank

Immediately after graduating from high school, I made a bold move. I enlisted in the Navy. It wasn't something I put a lot of thought into. I was young, concerned about getting my girlfriend pregnant and a prime target for the draft, so it just seemed like the right thing to do. I had no aspirations for higher education and thought at the very least the Navy might be able to help me lose weight and quit smoking.

Unfortunately, it didn't take long to figure out that military life wasn't for me—about 3 days, to be exact. In addition to having all my clothes taken away from me and relinquishing my HBO, I didn't particularly care for living in the same room with 40 strangers. I was never allowed to sleep in and I quickly discovered that I wasn't very good at taking orders. But, it did have one thing that made a lot of sense to me: uniforms and rank.

Since the beginning of time, the military has used uniforms and rank to identify people with special skills and seniority. Uniforms identify individuals who have earned distinction in their fields and respect amongst their peers by their experience, training and if nothing else, the raw stamina to put up with the military way of life. Of course, rank isn't always an accurate indicator of ability. As a seaman, I was constantly harassed by a new ensign who didn't know any more than I did. The only difference between the two of us was that he had the foresight to wait until after he graduated from college with a degree in drama before joining the military, where I didn't. As a reward for his higher education, he was given immediate command over the coffee mess, which included the responsibility of buying fresh glazed donuts for the likes of me. But, even if you didn't know them, you could always tell where other people stood just by looking at the uniform they wore.

After starting a new job last year and meeting dozens of people in rapid succession, I quickly became mired in so many acquaintances and names, that I quickly forgot who was who and what they did. Were they the CEO or a mailroom clerk? Did they instantly deserve respect or did they spend 20 years clawing their way up the corporate ladder? It occurred to me how helpful it would be if the civilian world adopted the practice of wearing uniforms and awarding ranks. It could start from the first day you were born.

Newborns would be awarded one stripe the minute they popped out of their mother's womb—sort of like the rank of Seaman Recruit in boot camp. The only thing you have to do to earn a Seaman Recruit's stripe is continue to breathe. For every phase of training you completed, you could earn another stripe: Seaman Apprentice for getting through grade school, Seaman for high school graduates, Ensign for finishing four years of college, Commander and Captain for master's degrees and Admiral if you earned a PhD. If you chose the other route and went to trade school, you could work your way up the chain of command from Petty Officer 1st class to Master Chief Petty Officer.

To help everyone understand your background and expertise, you'd probably wear an insignia on your shoulder: stay at home moms would sport a picture of a station wagon crammed with screaming kids. People in the world of finance would display a broken dollar sign. Teachers would wear a bullwhip and hookers might flaunt a used condom.

The richest and most significant people in the country like Bill Gates, Warren Buffett and Christy Walton would naturally wear gold shoulder boards and epaulettes with bullion fringe. People with management jobs would wear gold braided Citation Shoulder Cords and have the freedom to choose whatever headgear they wished from berets to campaign hats (known to many as "Smokey the Bear" hats), Jäger corps, Glengarry, Coonskin, Bearskin, Russian Military, Bicorne hats or a Pope's Mitre. For special occasions, it's likely everyone—from the lowliest enlisted man to the highest Admiral—would cast away their work uniforms for their dress attire that included white leggings, red sashes worn diagonally across the chest and possibly a Fez or Turban. Oh, and a sword.

Other merits used by the military are ribbons and medals of distinction. When I was in the Navy, they gave all of us a National Defense Service Medal after graduating from boot camp; a reward for letting an organization brainwash you in less than 12 weeks. It wasn't much, but it helped balance the nametag that I wore over the other pocket of my uniform. Over time, if you achieved your goals and demonstrated unparalleled leadership, you could accumulate quite a chest of fruit salad. These went along with the hash marks you wore on your sleeve to indicate how many years you'd been in military service. Civilian uniforms could have the same thing. In addition to the common awards like the Good Conduct Medal (which you received at your annual review), high school teachers could earn the Distinguished Service Cross and Combat Action Ribbons.

Second grade teachers would automatically be awarded the Congressional Medal of Honor: the highest award given to a civilian for "conspicuous gallantry and intrepidity at the risk of his or her life above and beyond the call of duty while engaged in an action against the youth of the United States," even though most of them would probably be awarded posthumously. Anyone stuck in a low paying job they hated but kept because they desperately needed the money would be eligible for a POW ribbon. Mothers would be awarded ribbons for having children—baby blue for boys and pink for girls—with silver oak clusters if they had twins, and gold oak clusters if they had triplets or more. Anyone successfully surviving a divorce would automatically be awarded a Purple Heart. People in the entertainment industry (like Elizabeth Taylor or Richard Burton) might earn 5 or 6 Purple Hearts before they died.

Of course, like any new policy, there would likely be complaints. For instance, enlisted civilians and low-ranking officers would have to salute senior officers in passing everywhere they went: at the supermarket, Walmart, the dentist's office and swap meets. Officers would be prohibited from fraternizing with enlisted personnel.

Today, if an employee turns out to be a bad apple, you just fire them and a month later they have another job, probably better than the one they left. With the new civilian uniform guidelines, employers would be free to ceremoniously strip the scofflaw of his rank and break his sword over their knee in front of the entire office staff, then drum him out of the building. When interviewing for a new job, the applicant would have to explain the frayed stitching and dark area where their stripes used to be, and why they only had half a sword. It could work the other way, too. If an employee struggled to single-handedly bring in the McAfee account, unit supervisors would have the authority to award them a field promotion and effectively outranking the no good creep they had to work for all last year.

I know it's unlikely that civilian companies will adopt the military tradition of uniforms, but it seemed to make a lot of sense to me when I was sent home for three days without pay for telling an off-color joke to our new Mormon Chief Financial Officer. I didn't know who she was. I thought she'd enjoy it.

I'll Never Forget the Time I Remembered

For the life of me, I can't remember what this essay was going to be about. That happens a lot when you get to be my age. You seem to forget even the simplest things like your home address, where you keep your money or why you're wearing your underwear on the outside of your pants. Of course, it wasn't always like that.

There was a time when my mind was a veritable sponge for anything that passed within 100 miles of my senses. I have very important things filed away—like that 1974 Big Mac marketing slogan, "Two all-beef patties, special sauce, lettuce, cheese, pickles, onions, all on a sesame seed bun," but even under the penalty of death, I can't identify a tenth of the U.S. state capitols, the names of America's founding fathers or any of the other things new U.S. immigrants are required to know before acquiring equal citizen status with me.

When I graduated from high school, I thought my days of mindless memorization were over. My boot camp drill instructor set me straight on that. He introduced me to the first of thousands of acronyms I'd have to memorize during the next several years.

Not knowing the difference between AIREVACCONFIRM and COMLANTAREACOGARD could have dire consequences for an 18-year-old lad, still trying to figure out how he got talked into military service in the first place. So, I just accepted it and learned how important COMLANTFLT, NAVMILPERSCOM and MIDRATS were going to be in my life.

As a pre-med major in college, I had to commit to memory every bone, ligament and muscle in the human body to get an 'A' in human anatomy. Even though that information still hasn't left me, it's been of little use to me as a bad boy in the neighborhood. I wish I could exchange the minute details about the ascending Loop of Henle for the lyrics to "California Love" by Tupac Shakur: "Out on bail, fresh outta jail, California dreamin' / Soon as I step on the scene I'm hearin' hoochies screamin'."

Over the years, I've been amazed at the sheer volume of space I've wasted cramming new lingua franca into my already dwindling cranial space. Every time I launch a new career, there's another lengthy list of terms I'm required to learn that don't have anything to do with the last. And I'm not the only one with complaints. According to my dentist, he doesn't use any of the terms he acquired in high school auto shop. If he had, it would make his job much easier: "Margie, how about handing me that 3/8-inch torque wrench with the 6-inch drive, so I can clean out Mr. Smith's root canal?"

In all fairness, it's not my brain's fault for failing to keep up with the incessant demand for retaining information. Between being submerged in beer during fraternity keg parties, oxygen-depleted by pot and suffocated with black market muscle relaxants, it's a wonder there's anything left for my dementia and Alzheimer's to grab on to. I haven't yet had to wrestle with Creutzfeldt-Jakob disease, prosopagnosia, fibromyalgia, hydroephalus, meningitis, Parkinson's disease, epilepsy or transient ischemic attacks but there have been plenty of times I've stood in the kitchen wondering why I walked in there in the first place. To avoid looking stupid in front of my girlfriend, I'll usually just grab the blender and take it back to the bedroom. My frequent irrational behavior has gotten to the point where she's learned not to ask questions anymore. She just makes room for another kitchen appliance on the nightstand.

Monkey in a Pink Canoe

At times, I wonder if I'm finally losing ground for good. As I get older, I've become aware of my attention fading in and out. I'll frequently stand in front of the ATM, trying to remember my 4-digit PIN, but all I can come up with is the theme song to "The Brady Bunch." While commendable, it still leaves me without any lunch money. I've forgotten so many passwords, I just write them on outside of my credit cards and hope nobody gets hold of my wallet. I buy Post-its by the case and label the contents of every drawer, box or opaque container with things that are important to locate sometime in the future—like this afternoon. I've also concluded that failing memory is the reason why all of the best chefs never write down any of their recipes. They'd simply never find them again. So, instead of referring to thick cookbooks, you'll usually see them grabbing handfuls of oregano, slinging it into a large bowl with a pinch of saffron and a smidgen of fenugreek.

Over the years, I've tried numerous approaches to retrieving information that's taken flight. On my doctor's orders, I've tried ways to stimulate my memory by getting more exercise, sleeping in the buff and learning how to laugh. He also suggested that I try varying my routines by eating while blindfolded, learning the sitar, changing my clothes every hour, conversing in Flemish and speaking to women in Braille.

I don't know where all my accumulated knowledge has gone since those first days, drooling in my bassinet. I keep stuffing it in but eventually, it just keeps seeping out—like air from an old inner tube. And, it doesn't seem to matter what type of thoughts I try to dredge up. Normally, I wouldn't mind losing a few principles of beginning Calculus. But, when I'm struggling to introduce my girlfriend to my brother, it can be a real problem when I can't remember her name—even after living with her for 5 years. They call those incidents "brainfarts," and they've been responsible for more than a few nights spent sleeping on the couch.

Eventually, I suppose it'll get so bad that someone will have to commit me to a nursing home; one of those places where they lock you in your room because you can't remember if your toothpaste goes in your mouth or in your ear; the places where they hang your spoon around your neck, so you won't lose it; the places where they tie your shoelaces together so when you feel like running, all you can do is shuffle to the next nurse's station. But, in the meantime, I'm doing pretty well by looking for the different colored tape on the floor and following it to the index card that tells me what to do next.

A Prescription for Struggle

When Dr. Lustgarten walked into the exam room holding the results of my physical, I knew it wasn't going to be good.

"Mr. Smith, I have good news and bad news for you."

"What is it? My cholesterol? Blood sugar? Has my Progeria or Tourette's Syndrome flared up again?" I knew it wasn't my Pica. I haven't had a craving for dirt or feces in over a year. And I swear, I've been meaning to get that colonoscopy, but I just haven't had time what with the parole hearings and all.

"No," said Dr. Lustgarten. "It's nothing that benign. Mr. Smith, I'm going to give it to you straight: you're fat. Dumpy. Roly-poly. Pudgy. Potbellied. Whale-like and a lard-ass."

I gasped. "How can that be? How fat am I?"

"Well, if your I.Q. was even half of what you weigh, I'd be submitting your name for Mensa membership. But fortunately, there is good news. According to the American Medical Association, obesity is now classified as a disease, which means that we can successfully treat it and your insurance company will cover the entire cost. I'd like to begin right away by admitting you to the ICU and conducting a full range of tests before it gets out of hand. We don't know how contagious you are, so I'm going to isolate you from all thin people."

"But, how did I get this way?"

"No one entirely understands obesity, but what we do know is that it manifests itself through a variety of clever mechanisms, deeply rooted in declining drive and low self-esteem. The first thing you probably lost after graduating from college was your interest in the uneven parallel bars. Instead of bicycling to work, you probably bought one of those senior scooters so you wouldn't have to walk from your car to the front door of your office. Ultimately, your boss agreed to let you work from home because of all the time you said you'd save, but we both know that you're just too lazy to get out of bed."

Obesity. I had no idea that I'd allowed myself to slide this far. The entire concept was impossible for me to get my arms around. Oh sure, I'll admit that my muffin top had gained a little momentum over the past year. But I knew lots of people who wore sweatpants to work. And, I was a little suspicious when the airlines charged me for *two* seats to Cleveland. But I had no idea that it had progressed to a medical disease worthy of AMA distinction.

I wasn't sure how to break the news to my close friends and family, so I posted a carefully worded entry on Facebook:

"Dear Friends. I know it's been a while since we've spoken, but I thought the time was right to personally break the bad news to you. Last week, I was diagnosed with a life-threatening disease manifested by extreme Häagen-Dazs abuse and underwear so tight that it cuts off the blood supply to my one-eyed wonder weasel. But, I don't want you to worry. I'm in good hands and should be fine after several excruciating liposuctions. I just wish I could say the say the same for you. My endocrinologist suggests that all of you who have come into direct contact with me since my sophomore year of high school make an appointment for a painful series of corpulence inoculations—especially if you're a woman over 40."

Monkey in a Pink Canoe

Within 10 minutes I received thousands of Tweets, emails and condolences: "I'm so sorry to hear to that you gained 40 pounds. My thoughts and prayers are with you." One even sent me a story about how he had beaten obesity and was in remission since the Superbowl. My office mate's gesture was sincere, even though misplaced. He sent me a 50-lb. basket filled with chocolate-chip cookies, cheese and wine. At least I could eat the balloons.

My therapist recommended that I embrace my disease through the 7 stages of grief: shock, denial, anger, bargaining, depression, testing and acceptance. I worked my way through shock even before I left the doctor's office. Then came denial.

It was easy to deny I'd become two of my former selves. But since I now knew that obesity is a disease and not something I'd brought on voluntarily, I wasn't too hard on myself. It wasn't *my* fault that I'm overweight. Like Kathy Bates, B.B. King, Oprah Winfrey and Michael Moore, I'm just big-boned. An article I'd read in Prevention Magazine confirmed it.

The next day bargaining and depression set in so I bought a dozen glazed Krispy Kremes on the way home from Weight Watchers. I made a deal with myself. If I could make it all the way home without opening the box, I'd cancel my membership. If I couldn't, I'd throw in the towel and return to class in the morning.

Since the AMA announcement, it was standing room only at Weight Watchers. Some of the heavier women had to sit on the floor because they couldn't wedge themselves into the regular classroom desks. After the meeting was over, it took three instructors and a fork lift to get them back on their feet so they could waddle up to the front of the class to pick up their meals. I opted to have all of my meals delivered directly to my home. I ended up eating an entire month's worth of food on the first day and they refused to send me more, so I quit.

I knew a couple of pencil-thin women from my days in Overeaters Anonymous. They committed themselves to OA after being diagnosed with Bulimia and Anorexia, so I thought they'd be a good source of information on how to lose a lot of weight quickly. As it turns out, both of those are considered diseases too, so their treatment would also be covered by my insurance if I got a note from my doctor. I'd tried starving myself before, so I knew Anorexia wasn't for me. Besides, I just didn't care one way or the other what I looked like. I was completely void of any self-image.

The next day I visited the pharmacy with a prescription from Dr. Lustgarten for Syrup of Ipecac. It's an emesis drug designed to help you vomit, which is a critical part of Bulimia. I've never been fond of throwing up, so I needed all the help I could get. Fortunately, the syrup was covered under my diagnosis, so I had nothing to lose— except hopefully, 30 or 40 pounds.

Dr. Lustgarten also insisted that I start exercising again, but I was reluctant to follow his advice. I joined a gym back in the 80s but quit after three weeks, largely because of the clothing. I could never find Lycra tights big enough to wear into aerobics class. Instead of making me look lithe and svelte, my legs looked like two Kielbasas supporting half a gallon of vanilla ice cream. I also hate to sweat because it means too many trips to the laundry. But the most important reason is conserving heartbeats. My cardiologist told me that the average male's heart will beat 2,333,664,000 during the 74 years he's on Earth—that's assuming he doesn't live longer than he's supposed to. Restricted to a little more than 2 trillion heartbeats in my lifetime, I don't want to needlessly piddle them away. After all, I might need them someday.

I'm so grateful to the American Medical Association for diagnosing me with a bonafide disease instead of expecting me to shoulder the responsibility of obesity all by myself. Like diabetes, cancer and Alzheimer's it's not my fault. I have a disease.

Bank Robbery Made Easy

It's almost Autumn and I've managed to fritter away my entire recreation fund on useless things like rent and utilities. I've also gone completely through my savings, 401(k), inheritance and most of my frequent flyer miles. Barring an unexpected windfall, I may have to start selling off body fluids and parts, or resort to getting a regular job. Or, rob a bank.

I've thought about robbing a bank before, but it's not easy to do when you live in a small town. After all, if it were, everybody would be doing it. There are a lot of unique deterrents. Just about everybody in town knows who you are and what you wear ("Oh, you mean the Smith kid… Margaret and Kenneth's boy who always wears that dirty baseball cap?"). And, unlike the 1930s, you can't just drive up to the front of the bank like Bonnie and Clyde—you have to use paid, public parking structures. Driving around and around in circles after you've heisted bags of cash sort of defeats the purpose of a quick getaway.

If you've never been arrested or spent any time in jail, learning how to pull a bank job can be challenging. It's not like you can take classes. I found learning how to rob a bank was particularly difficult because I've never spent any time associating with known felons. So, I made an appointment with the reference librarian at our local library to find out what she had to offer. I explained to her that I was looking for an easy-to-read, yet comprehensive guide about how to rob banks—sort of like "Robbing Banks for Dummies." She was very encouraging, asked a lot of intuitive questions, but ultimately, I decided to beat it after I saw her dialing 911. There's not much on the Internet, either. The only information I could find were dumb criminal stories that tell you what *not* to do, so I just extrapolated from there. One guy robbed a bank with a nametag on the front of his company shirt, so I'll make sure not to do that. After investigating other resources around town (like a couple of rough-looking cab drivers and a weekend carnival ride attendant), I decided to go home and glean as much as I could from old reruns of Miami Vice and Highway Patrol. The next thing I needed was a non-descript getaway car.

I walked into Enterprise Rent-a-Car and demanded the fastest Yugo they had for under $25. "And make sure it blends in with other traffic," I demanded. The girl behind the counter asked, "Would you like to take out insurance on your Yugo, Mr. Squatzengetzit?" I went ahead and took it because I figured there was a good chance that I'd be blowing out a couple of tires and sideswiping a police cruiser during the ensuing chase. I've never seen a get-away scene on television where they didn't and I certainly couldn't afford to pay for damage.

I didn't have a thing to wear to the bank robbery, so I stopped by The Robbery Store and picked up some dark gabardine pants, rubber-soled shoes, a pair of cotton work gloves and a Nixon mask. The clerk told me that it was one of his best sellers. "I've sold seven of them last week alone and a few of the robbers are still on the lamb."

I also bought one of those black SWAT jackets—the kind with a million pockets for your extra ammo, switchblade knife and flashlight, but I started getting concerned about wearing too many layers. Once you're inside the lobby, it's almost impossible to take off your jacket while holding an AK-47 on the clerks—and I hate to sweat—especially if circumstances erode into a hostage crisis and they turn off the air conditioning. The cops always do that. Right after they send in the pizzas.

I can't hop up on the counters as easily as I used to, so I'll probably have to bring one of those folding step stools from Home Depot. Great. Something else to carry. And I'm not going to forget the spray paint for the camera lenses. They almost blew that in Oceans 11.

Another bit of research that paid off was learning how to avoid dye packs. Dye packs are those pesky radio-activated units tellers slip between stacks of 10s and 20s that explode onto the would-be thief once they exit the bank. Well, I was way ahead of them. Instead of demanding the booty in paper currency, I planned on taking all of the money in loose change. Granted, it would be a little harder to lug out the door, but at least I wouldn't have to worry about ruining my new turtleneck sweater. I should still be able to wear it to my sister's wedding next month and I can always change the coins back into bills at the laundromat.

Three days before the job, my plans were dashed when some dufus beat me to the punch by getting caught robbing the same bank. Apparently, the heist was going smoothly until one of the customers pressed the panic button, thinking it was the customer service bell. The thief fled with $5 in small bills, traveler's checks and a pile of discount coupons for Costco. He was ultimately captured when he couldn't figure out how to unlock the driver's door.

Of course, there are lots of alternatives for making money other than robbing banks. Unfortunately, I can't think of them. I've never been successful working for other people because my dyslexia prevents me from following directions. I can't work for myself because I just don't have the discipline. I'm not artistic and don't have a musical bone in my body. That doesn't leave me with many options, except writing pieces like this—which is pretty much the same as robbing a bank, isn't it?

My Sizzling Russian Bride

By the time I found Svetlana, I knew I was in love. Having been tossed off all the run-of-the-mill American online dating sites like Farmersonly, GothicMatch, STDFriends, CougarWomen, Dirty-Encounters and Meet-an-Inmate.com, I finally resorted to trolling for eastern European women on SizzlingRussianBrides.com. That's where my troubles began.

After combing through thousands of profiles of beautiful Russian women, I settled on someone I thought could be the one. Svetlana was a voluptuous 27-year-old dental hygienist from the small village of Trochenbrod. According to her profile, she was college educated, spoke "some English" and loved reading, cooking, photography and pole vaulting. Her carefully crafted message read, "*Hi. I'm Svetlana. I'm womanly Russian single who is very communicable, counterbalanced and without bad habits. I like to meet lusty man in high social position to create family. I come from gay family, am sporty, well provided and would be orderly wife. I would love to make your intercourse.*"

For my part, I wrote an equally articulate profile that was meant to lure any eastern European woman into my web. I may have exaggerated a bit when I told her that I worked in the film industry, lived in Hollywood, hung out with Brad Pitt and never cheated on my mate. Largely because I was an unemployed extra, lived in NORTH Hollywood, drank every night with Bradley Pith, the janitor at my junior high school and couldn't cheat on my girlfriend because I've never had one.

While it was obvious that there were some cultural differences between the two of us, I decided to begin a relationship with Svetlana. I scoured the Internet for tips on how to put my best foot forward with a Russian woman. One site recommended learning some of her language, so I memorized a few terms like *privet, kak dilah, ochen kharasho, kak tiibya zovut, dah, niet* and *pakah*. To this day, I don't know what any of those mean, but it seemed to impress her that I tried. Another site said it was important to treat Russian women like ladies, "…as if you were looking after your 90-year-old grandmother…" That made a lot of sense to me, so I went out and bought her an aluminum walker and installed a raised toilet seat in the bathroom.

Over a year of Skype sessions, we used our hands, feet, some unusual facial expressions and a set of sixth grade flash cards to get to know each other. I'd ask her questions like, "How do you feel about having 15 children?" by trying to emulate a babushka scrubbing diapers by hand. In turn, she queried me on things important to her, like the size of my abdominals, how much money I made, what kind of car I drove, how much money I made, how far I lived from Beverly Hills and most importantly—how much money I made. I didn't have the heart to tell her the truth. Nonetheless, with such sound, mutually agreeable life-values, I proposed and flew Svetlana to the United States to start our new life together.

I met Svetlana's flight on a blistering southern California afternoon. By the time the TSA finished her cavity searches, it was time to take my new fiancé home to unpack and then out to dinner at Robert's Russian Cuisine—the Olive Garden of Soviet gastronomy. We spent the evening enamored in each other's glow. We hadn't discussed things like sleeping arrangements, so I broached the subject by laying salt and pepper shakers down on a napkin. "You, me make lovey tonight?" I asked. She thought I was giving her another present, so she wrapped them up and put them in her purse.

For the next few months, we spent all our time together. She brought some sort of bug over from Russia that had both of us flat on our backs making love to the porcelain goddess. On the bright side, you really get to know someone when they haven't taken a shower for more than a month and you're stuck in the house together, heaving your guts out. Eventually, I recovered and went back to seeing my friends, but she refused to leave the house. Svetlana spent the entire day on the couch, chatting with her old boyfriends on Facebook and making long distance phone calls to Trochenbrod. Most of my invitations were rebuffed with, "…when I learn English…" When we did go out, she had a wonderful time adding new American fashions to her wardrobe and annihilating the credit limits on my Visa, Mastercard, American Express and Home Depot cards. After we finally ran out of money, I suggested that it might be fun to stay indoors and play some entertaining games. I suggested Monopoly, Parcheesi, Candyland, Scrabble, Chutes and Ladders and hide the hot dog. Her favorites were DungeonQuest, Banzai Shuffleboard, Mahjong and Russian roulette with a glue gun.

When I discovered her aversion to cooking and cleaning, I broached the subject during dinner one night, thinking that she couldn't get too worked up if she was eating. She started to hyperventilate, cry, took all my Valium and ran into the bathroom where she stayed until the battery on her cell phone ran out. It was so painful not being able to use the toilet that I eventually capitulated and never brought the subject up again. It was easier just to do the vacuuming, cooking and laundry than risk getting another bladder infection.

I wish I could say that Svetlana and I are still together. She was a quick study. It didn't take her long to figure out that North Hollywood wasn't Beverly Hills, that I didn't know any actors and a Hyundai Accent was a long way from a Pagani Zonda. I came home one day after looking for work to an empty apartment and a carefully worded note: "*Ewrtfg xcewrtfg uypoiu jueroi dfpyert. Dfgert uio.*" That was the end of my sizzling Russian bride.

Don Ho Versus the Norwegians

From the moment my brother invited me to visit him on the north shore of Oahu, all I could think about was the fragrance of Hibiscus wafting through the evening air, miles of white sandy beaches, steel guitar and ukulele music and papayas growing in the front yard. What I hadn't thought about were the rats.

Besides being home to quaint Waikiki, Oahu is famous for its nightlife: 7 varieties of Geckos, 17 species of amphibians, dozens of poisonous lizards, snakes, spiders, frogs, toads, centipedes and the biggest rats known to man. Rats that carry fatal diseases like the plague, murine typhus, leptospirosis, and salmonellosis. Rats that can eat through linoleum floors faster than a cordless Makita.

My brother's house was in the country, on the point of Waimea Bay—literally a toad's throw from the water and the jungle they call home. Built in the early 1940s, none of the windows really shut. It was riddled with spaces between the clapboard siding, giving amphibious visitors unbridled access to the inside of his home. Tourists staying in Waikiki never learn about this elusive slice of

Hawaiian life because modern high-rise hotels are sealed tighter than a Wahine's pink canoe and constantly patrolled by exterminators.

The morning following my arrival, I learned my first lesson about living in the Hawaiian countryside: never leave dirty dishes in the sink until morning. We had partied well into the wee hours of the morning and were far too inebriated to even think about kitchen work, so I left a lasagna pan soaking in the sink, thinking I'd deal with it in the morning. As I lumbered into the kitchen, I was greeted by a family of orange-spotted geckos that had set up camp on the kitchen counter. They wanted to stay clear of the giant centipedes and 3-inch banana spiders getting their first taste of Italian food. Fortunately, they were as surprised to see me as I was to see them, so they dashed out a crack in the corner of the kitchen to tell all their neighbors there was a new chef in town. They'd be back tonight.

Then, I met the cane toads. During the rainy season, cane toads move from fields and sewer pipes to the damp darkness underneath the houses dotting the north shore. About the size of a child's softball mitt, they slept under our house during the day. When the sun went down, they came out by the hundreds, looking for bugs on our front lawn. Urban legend has it that cane toads ooze toxic secretions from their necks when they feel threatened. If you handle them correctly, you can lick or smoke the secretions for a cheap hallucinogenic high. I wasn't aware of this when I accidentally stepped on the back of one. Otherwise, I would have tried giving him a cheap hickie instead of throwing a loaded ice chest at him before sprinting back inside. It's hard to say who was more surprised—him or me. I do know who jumped the highest and promised himself never to walk outside after sunset without wearing ski boots.

With several valuable lessons under my belt about country living, I settled in for an extended stay and got ready to surf some of the best beaches in the world, until the scratching began.

My brother and I each had a bedroom in the two-bedroom house. Sharing a common bathroom, each bedroom was off to the side and had a door we closed at night for privacy. It also turned out to be effective rodent control.

Monkey in a Pink Canoe

One evening while dozing off to sleep, loud scratching on the linoleum floor, like the sounds your chemistry professor used to make on the chalkboard, awakened me. With both doors to the bathroom shut, it was obvious that a hairy interloper had found an alternative entrance into the bathroom from underneath the house, scratched around the room, then left the same way he came in.

I felt immediate relief after calling my brother's landlord. He knew exactly what the sound was and how to get rid of it. "You've got Norwegian rats that have burrowed into your bathroom," he said. "They come in through the floorboards in search of sugar cane, macadamia nuts, coffee, papaya and bananas." I assured him that we didn't keep any of those in the bathroom, but argued that the scent of toothpaste, deodorant and my bottle of English Leather could have attracted them. They did a pretty good job enticing the women I dated, so why shouldn't they work on a Norwegian rat? Then he added, "They're also motivated by thirst, hunger, sex, maternal instinct, and curiosity"—all the things that appeal to teen-aged boys—so I knew they weren't after coffee and bananas. "Go down and talk to Kimo at Haweiwa Hardware," he said. "He'll get rid of your rats."

Kimo had lived on the north shore his entire life and knew everything there was to know about getting rid of nasty Norwegians, at least the rodent types. "The best way to get rid of Norwegian rats is to trap them," he said, as he pulled out a mouse trap that could have stopped a bear. It measured 24-inches long and took two of us to cock. "The rats go for a slices of kosher hot dogs, dried papaya or mango, hickory-smoked bacon, organic peanut butter, Godiva chocolates and Margarita Jelly Bellies," so that ran me another $200 in bait. Evidently, rats have refined their tastes over the years from the days of Velveeta cheese.

That afternoon, my brother and I carefully baited the bathroom with 5 or 6 traps set with a lethal combination of hot dogs, bacon, peanut butter and candy. We figured if they didn't get caught in the trap, they'd eventually succumb to a heart attack from all the cholesterol we were feeding them. Just to be thorough, we left a cassette player running with Don Ho singing "Tiny Bubbles," thinking it would curdle their blood. Then, we closed the bathroom doors and went to bed.

About one o'clock in the morning I was awakened by a scratching sound, followed by a loud "SNAP!" I could have sworn I heard a high-pitched voice yelling out, "Uff da!" Ten minutes later, our Scandinavian visitor had kicked the rodent bucket.

Both of us knew we had reeled in our first Norwegian Brown. The problem was, neither one of us wanted to deal with a dead rat with a squashed neck and eyeballs popping out of his head. My brother needed to take a shower and get to work, so taking immediate command of the situation, he covered the dead vermin with a paper grocery bag, leaving it for me to deal with when my bladder got full enough to force me into the bathroom. It didn't work. I climbed out a window to pee and used the garden hose to brush my teeth, leaving Ole for my brother when he got home from the office.

Despite all our efforts at keeping the rats at bay, they managed to find ways into the bathroom, kitchen and dining room while we hunkered down under the covers, waiting for them to leave. After two weeks, the Norwegian rats won. I abandoned the hunting expedition and headed back to California, letting my brother deal with our hairy visitors. After all, it was his house. Or, should I say, *their* house?

New Horizons in Weight Control

During one of my recent nocturnal online shopping trips, I came across a number of great new products designed to make it easy to lose and manage your weight. Well, they hadn't actually become products yet, but were still in the "figment of someone's imagination" phase—based enough in reality to have been issued patents—but still miles away from seeing the light of day. I did, however, manage to find three that *were* for sale, so I scooped them up before they disappeared off the market.

Scientists and Registered Dieticians agree that most people are overweight because they eat too much, too fast. That's where the **Alarm Fork** comes in. This handy battery-operated utensil comes with two lights embedded in the handle: one green and one red. Sensors in the tangs of the fork tell it when it's loaded with food and turn the red light on. After you slide the empty fork out of your mouth, a built-in timer insures that the red light stays lit until you've had time to completely masticate and swallow your food. After a brief period of time, the green light on the handle comes on, letting you know that you're free to load up again.

I liked the Alarm Fork because it came calibrated from the factory according to my height, weight and metabolic rate, so it's impossible for me to override its settings or demand that it do more than it was designed to do. Whether I'm having a simple repast at home with my family or savoring my last meal on death row, the Alarm Fork continues to out-perform all its competitors. Not that there are many. It also comes with a number of exciting accessories, like disposable tangs, so I can take it with me when I dine out. After a meal, I just replace the used tangs and throw them away. It also comes with a smart looking imitation leather carrying case and sturdy belt clip, so I'll never have to wonder where I've misplaced it. There are even two extra slots for a knife and spoon.

If you're like me, you've probably tried to lose weight through dieting, exercise, drinking large quantities of water and holding your breath, but still manage to rack up the pounds. Just when I was ready to throw in the towel, I came across the **Mouth Cage**.

The Mouth Cage is so simple, it's a wonder no one has come up with the idea before. Well, actually, they have. Patterned after the device worn by Dr. Hannibal Lecter in the Academy-Award winning movie, "The Silence of the Lambs," the Mouth Cage is a scaled down version of the one worn by Hannibal the Cannibal and is light enough to be worn at the office, in church, school and at Overeaters Anonymous meetings. It's so attractive people forget I'm even wearing it.

I was instantly lured to its sturdy, stainless steel straps that hold the cage across my mouth. It's secured in place with a bulletproof padlock, making it impossible to eat anything after I put it on in the morning. The cage is constructed from a series of thin stainless steel wires that crisscross and cover my entire mouth. Once applied, the only way I can remove it is with the proper key. Even lock and key technicians can't get it off.

Unlike its competitors, the Mouth Cage is both functional and attractive enough to envelop my entire mouth, while still allowing me to speak, laugh and smile but not eat, drink, smoke, spit or vomit. At the end of the day, my Weight Watchers sponsor removes the device so I can put it in the dishwasher, insuring that it's sparkling clean in the morning.

At first, I was concerned about how the cage looks and how my friends and co-workers would receive it. Fortunately, the Mouth Cage comes in a variety of festive colors and designs so it matches whatever I'm wearing. It's even available in a beautiful, stainless-steel model with a lustrous chrome finish for those special occasions like weddings, funerals and the Academy Awards. Managing my diet has never been easier!

Even as effective as the other products are, there are times when I still cave into temptation. For those particularly difficult times, it's nice to know that help is on the way with the **Oral Alert**. This handy device looks just like a wristwatch, and it is. But besides being able to tell the time, this amazing device will prevent me from engaging in compulsive behaviors like overeating, smoking, drinking, snorting cocaine or sucking my thumb. Here's how it works.

The Oral Alert incorporates space age technology using three, axis attitude sensors that are programmed to sound an ear-splitting alarm and disable all electrical devices and cell phones within 50 meters any time my hand comes within an inch of my mouth. But, it still allows me to program several "free periods" during the day when it's alright to bring my hand near my face, such as brushing my teeth in the morning, eating breakfast, lunch and dinner. It also allows me to override two emergencies like sneezing or picking my nose. Being particularly void of will power, I went ahead and ordered two Oral Alerts— one for each wrist.

Like its cousin, the Mouth Cage, the Oral Alert is designed to be attached and secured in the morning by my therapist. In the event that I need to remove them during the day to play water polo or visit the emergency room, each device contains remotely operated circuitry so that my wife, parole officer or law enforcement official can unlock them using a PC or iPad. There's even a handy app designed for iPhones.

Since finding the Alarm Fork, Mouth Cage and Oral Alert, losing and managing my weight has never been easier. I no longer have to subject my family to all of those fad diets, extreme exercise regimens and expensive medical procedures. I just sit back and watch the pounds melt away!

A Little Baggage Never Hurt Anyone

I was a cute baby. I have the pictures to prove it. Lying there all alone in my bassinet, about the worst thing anyone said about me was I gurgled and filled twice as many diapers as the other kids. But, somewhere along the line, things must have changed. I've been accused of having baggage.

For the record, I'm not completely sure what everyone means by baggage. All three of my therapists agree that I don't have any baggage. I have issues. My psychiatrist insists I don't have issues. I've merely built an impenetrable wall around myself in response to being misunderstood by the rest of society. My parole officer says I'm not misunderstood. I'm just a weak-willed twit and I should get on with serving the remainder of my sentence.

As far as I can tell, I started picking up baggage as a First Grader. My brother told me not to eat anything that was green, that they had boogers in them. So, much to my mother's chagrin, I stopped eating green beans, collard greens, asparagus, broccoli, Brussels sprouts, all types of lettuce and anything with mold on it. To this day, I can't get within 200-feet of a salad bar without taking a

Valium. Then came slimy foods, anything raw, artificially colored or processed.

As I've matured, I've learned that just about everyone has baggage, so I'm not too hard on myself about mine. When I went away to my first summer camp, I was horrified by the temper tantrums Milton Hirsch threw until the staff caved in and gave him the lower bunk by the window. He flung himself on the floor and began thrashing about until he cracked his helmet. Normally, I wouldn't have thought too much about it, but he was the head counselor and was supposed to be setting an example for the rest of us. Taking note of his success, I figured out that the way to get what I wanted was to howl uncontrollably, rock back and forth and threaten to vomit on anyone that touched me. Those techniques have worked so well, I've continued to use them at the office and at my monthly court appearances. They'll also get you to the head of the line at the DMV and Costco.

Telling lies is a form of baggage I prefer over admitting the truth. But they've complicated my life to the point where even I'm not sure what the truth is anymore. So I've learned just to cover them up with more lies until it takes an Egyptologist to get to the facts.

Facebook, email, text messaging and online dating sites have been wonderful tools for generating baggage. Through blatant deception, I've successfully manufactured dozens of fictional personalities that work until I'm forced to actually meet someone face to face. By that time, we're both so sick of trying to distinguish fact from fiction that it's easier just to accept the good with the bad and keep plowing ahead.

With divorce rates as high as they are, people have learned to be on the lookout for red flags: baggage that is death knells to long-term relationships. Even I've accepted that while most people you meet these days are immature, volatile, unpredictable and selfish, it's all just a matter of degrees. People are much more inclined to accept your minor faults if they suspect you're hiding something much more serious like a prison record or sex change. To keep things simple, I make it a point to demand the same dinner every night: a Swanson's Salisbury steak dinner, served at room temperature. I have to eat at exactly 5:30 PM, facing north with a white, plastic spork. If it's late, I'll refuse to eat and just sit there, rocking back and forth, staring at my plate. It makes going out to eat so challenging, people will usually overlook all of my other shortcomings and rush to get me seated at the restaurant before the sun goes down.

All in all, I consider myself someone who's upfront and easy to live with, despite the fact that I don't fly, take trains or travel by any means other than ambulance. Even then, I have to take several Thorazines just to see a movie. I don't like snow or the beach and consider laughter a sign of weakness. Other than that, I'm a pretty easy person to get to know as long as you never try to pry the remote control out of my hands.

While some people have labeled me defensive, controlling, insecure, impotent and ignorant of good hygiene practices, I contend that they just haven't taken the time to get to know me. Let's face it. It's hard work making important relationships function when you've committed your life to unfounded suspicions. But, I'm always open to building a solid relationship based on fear and jealousy and I'm surprisingly accommodative to a little backstabbing.

It's been a while since I've met someone who has been open minded enough to accept my baggage, not that I'm admitting I have any. I keep meeting people with the same unrealistic expectations: people who crave happy, healthy relationships void of insecurities, a house with a white picket fence, 2.5 children, a station wagon in the garage, an active Match.com profile and thousands of friends on Facebook. Unfortunately, I guess I'll always be the one stuck standing at the airport, looking for an opportunity to offload some of my baggage. Any takers?

Better Living through Drug Addiction

I'm hopelessly addicted to drugs. You name a pill, syrup, lotion, cream, antacid, vitamin, tranquilizer, hormone, douche or suppository and I've not only taken it, but I've abused it, largely because I have an addictive personality. Anything worth taking is worth taking a lot.

In all fairness, I can't assume the blame for my wayward behavior. It began the day I popped out of my mother's womb when the pediatric nurses started basting me with petroleum jelly and baby lotion like I was a Thanksgiving turkey. In those days, babies were always covered with something. Pediatricians were convinced by the drug companies that it was dangerous for a baby's skin to come in direct contact with the air or sunlight without a protective layer of gook. Then came the decongestant drops and saline nasal sprays they shot up my nose, which would come in handy years later when I got addicted to cocaine.

Expectant mothers today are lucky if they spend 24 hours in the maternity ward. Doctors recommend that new dads just leave the engine running. Thanks to new insurance guidelines, babies are delivered faster than you can lance a boil. When I was born, new mothers were allowed to wile away a week or more in the hospital after giving birth before they were sent home. That gave newborns plenty of opportunities to get strung out on all sorts of drugs and be exposed to leprosy from the guy down the hall. There wasn't much to do in the pediatric ward as a child, so I started smoking cigarettes and hanging out with a rough bunch of newborns in "The Cribs." We were constantly in trouble with the staff for soiling our diapers, spitting up our breakfast and peeing on people whenever they picked us up. By the time I left the hospital, I was hopelessly strung out on the Pedialyte they gave me to counter the dehydration from a week of projectile vomiting and diarrhea.

At home, I wrestled with the normal challenges of crib life: rashes, colic, gas from my bottle. You name it. Then, came the teething. My mother didn't have a clue how to get me to stop crying until my grandfather wandered into my nursery and rubbed my gums with some of his Jack Daniels. I loved it and stopped crying immediately. I loved it so much so that I voluntarily extended my teething process for several more years. By that time I had developed a serious drinking problem and ended up doing the first pediatric stint at the Betty Ford Clinic.

After getting out of rehab, I progressed through the usual childhood diseases—measles, mumps, chickenpox, rubella, hepatitis A and B, pertussis, polio, rotavirus, blaschko's lines, meningitis, scurvy, leprosy, cholera, elephantitis, rickets, bubonic plague, blue skin disorder, pica, tourette's syndrome, rubella, tetanus, tuberculosis, scarlet fever, Alice in Wonderland syndrome, mononucleosis and jumping Frenchman's disorder—all the usual stuff. It seemed each disorder required its own prescription lotion, salve, powder or goo that I was instructed to take for the rest of my life.

As an adult, I've continued the tradition of making sure that I take *something* every day. And, I'm not alone. According to the Department of Health and Human Services, over 70% of Americans take at least one prescription drug daily. Sure, I may get up feeling fine, but I can't afford risking the possibility that I *might* feel bad later in the day. I could get a headache at work or dysentery from drinking out of the backyard garden hose. My blood pressure and glucose could shoot up, or they could plummet through the floor. Whatever happens, I don't want to spend one minute more in pain than I have to. If there's a drug out there to mask my discomfort, I want it in vast quantities.

In the old days, none of this would have been a problem. I'd have died well before I started contracting all the diseases associated with getting old. My lean frame would have probably succumbed to pushing my covered wagon up a snow-congested pass. If that didn't kill me, the attacking Indians probably would. Or, I could have been fatally wounded by a grizzly bear before reaching 35. Today, I'm more likely to die from a heart attack in my cubicle while eating a chocolate éclair.

Thanks to preventative medicine, I'm now hooked on more drugs than at any other time in my life. I probably will be for another 30 years. Each morning begins with vitamins A, B, C, D and E. I also take acytyl carnitine, chromium, cod liver oil, DHEA, fish oil, folic acid, lavender, phenylalanine, rhodiola, St. John's wort and tyrosine. I eat all my meals out of the vending machine down the hall, so I take Crestor and niacin tablets to manage my cholesterol and some fast-acting fiber tablets to keep things moving. I quit smoking 30 years ago, so I chew Nicorette gum just in case I get the urge to start again. My knees hurt from being so overweight, so I coat them with a generous layer of Bengay and cover my shoulders, elbows and lower back with Salonspa patches. Being so dependent on all these depresses me, so I take double doses of Elavil, Welbutrin, Cymbalta, Lexapro, Prozac, Tofranil, Paxil, Zoloft, Desyrel and Effexor just to get through the day.

If you include everything I put in my mouth, on my skin, up my nose and in my eyes, the cost of better living through chemistry runs me thousands of dollars each year. Oh sure, I could probably stop taking most of them, but why should I? I can't afford to suffer for one minute more than I have to. As long as there's a drug out there that will make me feel different, I'll take it. It doesn't even have to be better, just different. As Dr. Timothy Leary once said, "Uh, whatever."

Alcohol Of Fame

Buying a case of beer always seemed to be a problem. Leading the sheltered life of a 16-year-old from the San Fernando Valley, I didn't want heroin, uppers, downers, roofies, opium, cocaine, ecstasy, LSD, steroids, crack cocaine, PCP or pot. I wasn't even interested in vodka, whiskey or tequila. All I wanted was a case of beer.

The way I usually found it started on Wednesday, by putting the word out to all my friends to check with their connections. Later that day I'd discover an anonymous note in the bottom of my school locker from a dealer.

I spent the next three hours following directions that put the Lindbergh kidnapping case to shame. I tossed the beer into the trunk of my car, where it stayed until Friday night, warming up to the temperature of a certain kidney byproduct from an equestrian animal—and similar in taste. There had to be an easier way to get a cold beer. As it turned out, there was. His name was Stan.

Stan was a huge guy for only being a junior in high school. He was 6 foot 4, weighed 235 and wore size 17 Converse high-tops. Because of his bulk, he was able to get a job working behind the counter at his uncle's liquor store in an affluent part of town. I could buy whatever I wanted from Stan and it was easier than the black market. The down side was that I had to include him in all my activities. But, that turned out to be advantageous. I'd dress Stan in a black suit and tell all the girls he was my bodyguard.

Later, I stepped up (or down, depending on how you look at it) to cheap wine and found that buying alcohol was largely a matter of supply and demand. If you could find a decrepit enough liquor store that was desperate for your money, they'd sell you anything. Since I was never interested in taste, I'd hit the bargain bins in the back corner of the store. Bargain bins were filled with unknown brands of clearance wines that no one else in their right mind would think about buying, let alone drinking. Brands like Bartles & Jaymes, Blue Nun, Mad Dog 20/20, Boones Farm, Cisco, Ripple, Old Smiley, Night Train Express, Thunderbird, Arriba and 777 Russian Port Wine and All-Purpose Wallpaper Remover.

As luck would have it, I was taking a public speaking class in junior college. Our mid-term assignment was to deliver a 10-minute speech on how to make something. One of the students brought in an empty gallon bottle and poured in grape juice, sugar and yeast. He sealed the top with a condom and promised that we'd be drinking some of the most memorable wine of our lives by the end of the semester when he gave his final speech. We did. We got so wasted that the professor cancelled the last half of the class and sent everyone home to sober up. That was at 10:00 in the morning. And they say you never learn anything in college…

Over time, I graduated from cheap beer and wine to even cheaper spirits. The point was never to enjoy their taste. The goal was to get as drunk as possible in the shortest amount of time. I grew to love Popov vodka and the cheap gin they sold at Fedco. When feeling rambunctious, my friends and I would pile into my VW bug and drive south to Tijuana. While you could easily buy Mexico's name brand tequila for a fraction of what it cost in the U.S., we tended to gravitate to the off-label torpedo juice. You could find it at gas stations in refilled Pepsi bottles, sealed with a cork and melted wax. No label, no identification of any kind to indicate what was inside. Just 100% grain alcohol guaranteed to melt the rims off your glasses. To this day, I blame it for my never becoming a Rhodes Scholar.

I'm older now and quit drinking years ago. After experimenting with all those variations of cheap booze and every recreational drug known to mankind, I've learned to enjoy the magical wonders of reality. It's so much more fun waking up in the morning, remembering what you did the night before, where you parked your car and not having to explain all the blood stains to your mother. And I don't have to entertain Stan.

Minutes from Lorraine

I was 5 minutes away from becoming Lorraine.

During the period affectionately known as the Baby Boom, routine amniocentesis and maternal sonograms were still years away. And while the 50s and 60s can claim fame to some of the best music in the history of the universe, its struggling medical practices offered no help to new parents trying to choose a name for their children.

That being the case, one would think the prudent thing to do would be to spread your bets equally across two columns of names: one for boys and one for girls. But my parents were so convinced that I was going to be a girl, they put everything on pink and let it ride. When I finally did appear, I was a surprise to everyone—even me. I wasn't a girl.

Nowadays, new parents can avoid some of the stress of choosing a name by asking for the sex of their new baby weeks or months ahead of his or her arrival. While it does narrow down the naming choices by 50%, it still doesn't make the task any easier. In Germany, new parents get help from the government by requiring strict conventions that insure that a child's name is consistent with the baby's gender. The name can't be interpreted as being offensive or ridiculous (a practice the United States has yet to embrace) and its spelling must be conventional, probably to avoid any little Aedolfs running around Marienplatz in dresses.

Arab countries go one step further by dictating that newborn names adhere to religious values. Whether boy or girl, their middle names must contain a traditional moniker that honors the Prophets, so chances are you won't find many Fifi Trixibells or Pomegranate Purples destined for high public office. In China, fathers have the final say. And like the Arab culture, a Chinese newborn can have up to three names—one of them being a "generational" name such as Banpaizi, Ziyn or Chuanshizilian—something that rolls off the tongue when positioned next to their given name, Skipper or Buffy.

American parents resent anyone telling them what they can or cannot name their children—evident by the creativity of the celebrity parents of Bronx Mowgli (Ashlee Simpson and Pete Wentz), Moxie CrimeFighter (Magician Penn Jillette), Nakoa-Wolf Manakauapo Namakaeha Momoa (Lisa Bonet and Jason Momoa) and Spec Wildhorse (John Cougar Mellencamp and Elaine Irwin). What parents do demand is the freedom to give their children names that will espouse a lifetime of dignity, character and distinction, like Cholera Priest, Envy Burger, Pickle Parker, Gonorrhea and Syphilis (twins), Banana Howdy or Bart Simpson's favorites, Al Coholic, Anita Bath or Oliver Chlothesoff.

Short of using an iPhone App (yes, they do exist), there are a number of things to keep in mind when naming your newborn. Remember that they're going to have their names for the rest of their lives. Unless, of course, they decide to change them from Chad Johnson to Ochocinco, Maurice Micklewhite to Michael Caine, Issur Danielovitch Demsky to Kirk Douglas or Chaim Klein Witz to Gene Simmons. If they're musically inclined, your child may go from Leonard to Lil' Scrappy, Dreaddy Kruger, Cunninlynguists, Gnarls Barkley, Messy Marv, Chali 2na or Shorty Shitstain. When they get older, they can abbreviate their name to just their initials: JC (Jesus Christ), P. T. Barnum, L. L. Bean, J. K. Rowling, H.G. Wells or O. J. Simpson.

Some new parents bestow honor on a newborn by extending the legacy of their family tree. They'll choose great-great grandfather Elmer or one of his cousins, Lester, Homer, Cleveland or Nellie Belle— not that there's anything wrong with Lester, Homer, Cleveland or Nellie Belle—just as long as it flows when put next to the family name: Pickle Parker Cleveland Roosevelt.

Most pediatricians advise new parents to forgo coming up with creative spelling of their children's names: Kayciance-Clarita Jayne, Aksel Rhose, Razziel, Prinzstohn, Phenway, Benjerman, Dierrah and Jerzey Chor. Try to imagine your daughter who has now grown into a successful, 37-year-old prospective homebuyer on the telephone with her mortgage broker: "Yes, that's spelled, K-a-y-c-i-a-n-c-e... Just like it sounds."

Keep in mind what's going to happen to their initials or monograms, once they become rich and powerful and have their clothes tailor-made. All of William Terrance Franklin's dress shirts will be emblazoned with WTF on the cuffs. Petunia Ursula Samuels' Armani suits will have PUS on the lapels. And, heaven help Farleigh Udell Keaton.

Think twice before saddling your children with cute nicknames that will haunt them until the end of time. While Cupcake, Pookie Bear and Snookums might seem like an affectionate way to start your kid down the road of life, chances are their classmates will replace them with their own merciless versions like WingNut, Four-eyes, Stumpy or Pizza Face that will inevitably haunt them until they achieve high political office: "Ladies and gentleman, the Speaker of the House, Ferret-face Fenstermacher."

Finally, there are few things in life worse than a man being given a woman's name. While it didn't seem to hurt the careers of Leslie Nielsen, Lindsay Buckingham, Evelyn Waugh or Stacy Keach, it's a guaranteed way to get your kids beat up in the parking lot of P.S. 496, so invest early in those Karate lessons. Similarly, if you're going to name your kids Winterby, Leighton or Chumley, you'd better be rich and be able to chauffeur them from private school in a bulletproof limousine. Otherwise, they'll never make it home alive.

With time running short and my mother anxious to checkout of her room, I still didn't have a name. So my father initiated a frantic inventory of items in the hospital room hoping for a good name for an 8-pound baby boy. Q-tip, emesis basin and sphygmomanometer were possibilities, but my mother would have nothing to do with it. Finally, he spied a Welch Allyn Vaginal Specula hanging on the wall. Two of the words were possibilities. He ultimately decided on Allyn. And, just to avoid saddling me with a lifetime of misspellings, he changed the spelling from Allyn to Allen. But I'm thinking of changing it to Lorraine.

Dealin' Delbert's Fine Used Babies

By the time I'd been crawling around the house for 3 or 4 years, my parents were already thinking about giving me a brother. My mother enjoyed being a stay-at-home mom and my auto mechanic dad was looking years ahead to the practical aspects of having another child: more cheap labor for the weekly chores. Unfortunately, my mother had such a tough time with my delivery, she didn't think she could go through it again and thought adopting a baby brother was the way to go.

"Are you sure?" asked my dad. "When you buy a used baby, you never know what's wrong with it until you get it home. Who was the previous owner? How well did they maintain him? Has he been in any accidents, and if so, how badly was he damaged? You can't tell just by looking at him."

He had a good point. Fortunately, there were services available that took a lot of the guesswork out of adopting a baby. My parents spent several evenings visiting local orphanages looking for used babies. While they knew they couldn't afford a brand new one, a 2 or 3-year-old kid was well within their means. "What about an older child?" asked my cost-conscious mom. Maybe something in the 12 to 14-year-old range?" "Absolutely not," exclaimed my dad. "By the time a kid gets to be that age, there's always something wrong with him. Oh sure, they'll gussy him up by giving him a haircut, a shower and a new set of clothes, but you never know what kind of mileage is on them once they reach that age. Once they get to be 12, they start breaking all their bones and leaking fluids. They might have even rolled back their birth certificate to make them look younger."

Another good point: The only sure way to know what kind of kid you were really adopting was to get him while he was young, before he racked up a lot of miles, crashed his tricycle, needed braces or had the Chickenpox, Croup, Rickets, Measles, Mumps, Osgood Schlatter Disease, Whooping cough or Scarlet fever. "Hell," said my dad. "They might have even patched-up a cleft pallet, tetralogy of Fallot or Prune Belly Syndrome." He was right. You just never know.

My mother had also considered going abroad to adopt one of the thousands of adorable children from China, Japan or Ethiopia. My father wouldn't have anything to do with it. "I'm not letting any little foreign job into this house. Besides, imported models are so hard to maintain. First, there's locating the parts. Then there's finding someone qualified to work on them, not to mention the expense. A friend of mine had a little Fiat that just about ran him into the poor house." My mother reminded him that we were talking about a child and not an Italian sports car, but he still wouldn't have anything to do with it. This family was going American.

After months of trolling Littledroolers.com, they picked out three babies to look at from Dealin' Delbert's Fine Used Babies: Chaim, Eshkol and Matityahu. They finally settled on Chaim because his name in Hebrew means "Life" which would probably work out better than Eshkol (meaning "cluster of grapes") or Matityahu which translates to "Gift from God." Nobody wants to be the parents of a Fifth Grader walking into the first day of class with a name like "Gift of God." It could be rough.

Finally, the big day came. Time to go out and meet little Chaim. Chaim was a beautiful 18-month-old boy with dark hair and large,

Monkey in a Pink Canoe

inquisitive eyes. My father didn't quite know how to handle the negotiations, so he just poked Chaim in the chest a few times with his index finger and lightly kicked his legs to see how well he maintained his balance. Then Dealin' Delbert reminded him that this was a child and not a used Plymouth. "How's his suspension?" my dad asked him. "Has he been in any wrecks recently? Can I see a copy of his Babyfax report?" My father was determined not to be duped into assuming someone else's problems. On the other hand, my mother fell instantly in love with little Chaim, so she made preparations to take him home. A new little baby brother!

While my mother was cooing over Chaim, my dad got down to brass tacks. He took Dealin' Delbert aside and asked, "So, how much is this little bundle of joy going to cost us? What kind of a warranty does he come with, and for how long?" Delbert assured him that they had selected an excellent child. "Chaim just had all of his shots and comes with a 2-year limited warranty, which covers all parts and major repairs to his drive train. We just gave him his 18-month transfusion and will even throw in a gift certificate for a free circumcision with the Moyle of your choice." That sealed the deal. They drove little Chaim home.

Apart from the incessant crying and projectile vomiting, which I understand is normal for children his age, Chaim has been a bundle of joy. My father has warmed to the idea of having an adopted son and my mother has finally started leaving him home long enough to stand in as goalie for my indoor hockey games.

If you would have told me a year ago that I'd have a cute little adopted brother, I wouldn't have believed it. But Chaim has become an inseparable part of the family. He'll be able to help around the house a lot more once I teach him how to operate the weed whacker, but that might be a couple of months from now.

Feng Shui-ing My Chakras

Dr. Levenfish was baffled. There was nothing more western medicine could do to effectively pull me out of the depths of my depression. True, the Prozac and marijuana helped, but they also contributed to my obesity, which made me feel even more disconsolate. Feeling like my life had totally unraveled, I began entertaining thoughts of self-immolation and non-traditional methods of suicide like handcuffing myself to my mother-in-law for the weekend. But I never had the courage to follow through with any of them. In desperation, Dr. Levenfish finally capitulated.

"Well, since you've made the decision to live, I guess we should start looking at alternative solutions. Have you ever thought about trying Chinese medicine?" he said. "There are a lot of interesting options that could be of help to you. Herbal medicine, Tantric massage, Qigong or acupuncture. Something that might correct your maligned Chakras."

I gasped. Up until now, I didn't even know I had Chakras, let alone the possibility that something could be wrong with them. Of course, that led to an infinite number of questions: how do you x-ray defective Chakras? Are they covered under my health plan? Will they apply to my deductible? What if I need a replacement—how hard is it to find a Chakra donor? It's certainly nothing my family talked about when I was growing up. Maybe we should have.

Dr. Levenfish was concerned enough about my suicidal tendencies to rush me over by ambulance to one of his colleagues, Dr. Wu Jian Huang. Dr. Huang was an esteemed practitioner in the art of Chinese medicine and had published hundreds of articles in such respected medical journals as Good Housekeeping, Woman's World and Redbook.

When the EMTs brought me in, the receptionist immediately snapped into action: she confiscated my clothes, charged my credit card for an office visit and handed me a 6-page health history questionnaire with the usual questions:

1. Under which moon were you born?

2. Please circle the Chakras related to your visit: Sahasrara, Ajna, Vishuddha, Anahata, Manipura, Swadhisthana, Muladhara.

3. Indicate which Chakras below the muladhara that are causing you problems: Atala, Vitala, Sutala, Talatala, Rasatala, Mahatala or Patala.

4. Which do you prefer: burial at sea or cremation?

After fifteen minutes, Dr. Huang came into the room. "Good morning, Mr. Smith. Dr. Levenfish called me and is concerned about your condition, so with your permission, I'd like to immediately begin examining your Chakras, Chi and meridians." I had no idea what he was talking about. For all I knew, he could have been saying, "早上好，史密斯先生。利文菲什博士給我打電話，是有關你的情況，所以我想與您的許可權，不浪費時間在探索你的脈輪，志和經絡" Which, of course, he was.

When he was finished, Dr. Huang pondered the ceiling and said, "Mr. Smith, I'll be honest with you. You're the worst case I've seen in 30 years of medicine. Nonetheless, I have good news and bad news. I'll give you the bad news first."

"Your female kundalini has somehow become disassociated from your male shiva which is negatively impacting your universal consciousness and unity. Your Manipura is producing conflicting feelings of fear, anxiety and panic attacks. Your Crown Chakra has completely shut down and is no longer drawing in energies from the Universal Life Force."

"What's the good news?"

"The good news is I think we can correct most of your issues through out-patient Chakra therapy and working with a Feng Shui expert." So, Dr. Huang wrote me a prescription for 12 visits to the Kamala Chanda Vitality Center. He would have written it for more, but the Vitality Center was out of network.

My therapist's name was Seeta Kajal. "We'll begin by re-aligning your Crown Chakra," said Seeta. "Have you been plagued by feelings of living in the past and being disconnected from the outside world?" I told her I had, so in addition to beginning a daily regimen of prayer and meditation, she instructed me to cancel my Facebook account. "I want you to stop focusing on how successful all of your high school classmates have become and what a pathetic mess you've made of your own life."

My heart Chakra also needed extensive therapy, which was manifested by depression, issues with trust and a total lack of confidence. "Begin by doing the breast stroke every day in the shallow end of a swimming pool to open up your heart," said Seeta. "If you don't have access to a pool, just use your toilet."

"People with mal-aligned Heart Chakras frequently distance themselves from physical contact with others." I told her that made a lot of sense. During my ten years in San Quentin, the only time I hugged anyone was during knife fights in the showers. So she recommended I begin and end each day by hugging myself. She was adamant that I not touch anyone. I'd have to work up to that over several years.

To resurrect my creativity, fertility and sex appeal, Seeta pressed on my second Chakra, located directly beneath my belly button. "Your second Chakra is blocked—which is why you're having problems with money, sex and your uterus." When I told her that I didn't think I had a uterus, she turned bright red and realized she had been referring to the wrong patient chart for our entire therapy session, but rather than own up to her mistake, she glossed over her error by driving me home to start my Feng Shui therapy.

"Feng Shui stands for 'wind' and 'water' and is the ancient art and science that reveals how to balance the energies in your living and work spaces, insuring that they synchronize with your Chakras," said Seeta. "Why don't you start by showing me your home?"

"Since my divorce, I've been renting this 6 by 12 lean-to behind my parents' house. It's not much, but it has everything I need: a sink, small bed and a hot plate where I cook all my meals. Next week, I'm planning on getting floor covering."

After she regained consciousness, Seeta explained in layman's terms the importance of maintaining a balanced Chi—the universal energy force that permeates virtually everything around us and is dependent on the delicate balance of the Yin and Yang. "In terms of universal energy," she said, "Yin represents soft, passive rhythms with feminine energy. I want you to surround yourself with soft music, soothing, relaxing art images and perhaps the sound of gentle, running water. In your case, you can use your annoying toilet with the broken flap valve."

"Yang is represented by strong, active energy that is characterized by vibrant bright lights, explosive colors and upward moving energy that contrasts the relaxed, diffused, passive Yin energy." So, she suggested that I paint the interior of my room day-glow orange and start inviting large groups of friends over for elaborate dinner parties. Within minutes, I could begin to feel the difference—my cluster headaches returned and I had three crippling grand mal seizures.

"Finally," said Seeta, "I'd like to examine your Bagua." So, without hesitation, I lowered my trousers. "No, no," said Seeta. "Your Bagua is a map of the inside of your home. We're looking for negative energies that impact the Chakras of your living space. Or, in your case, this crappy little hovel you call home."

We laid a Bagua grid over a schematic of my living quarters and positioned the lower end of the grid over the door. "Your 'Fame and Reputation' area should always face south" – the same place my parents stored all of the trashcans until I rolled them out to the curb on Thursdays. "The southeast Feng Shui area is connected to the flow of money energy in your life." That was adjacent to the compost pile and where we buried the dog's meadow muffins, so I could see that I'd have to make a couple of changes.

Seeta suggested that I surround myself with things that reminded me of better times. "It could be something as simple as a picture of your ex-wife walking along the beach, holding hands with her new millionaire husband and their beautiful children," she said. "Or, perhaps a memorable photo of where you spent your honeymoon," which happened to be the oil fields of North Dakota. By the same token, she told me never hang a mirror over my bed. "The worst thing you can do is subject yourself to your own reflection, first thing in the morning."

After 20 minutes, Seeta admitted that she had done everything she could do to correct the energy flow in my miniscule hovel and was anxious to leave. As she drove off, my parents came by, asking who the Asian lady was that just left my trailer. My mother thought she was a hooker and was ecstatic that I was taking steps to invigorate my sex life.

"No, no. That was Seeta," I said. "She's a Feng Shui expert and was here to adjust my Universal Energy flow and synchronize my Chakras." I told them about the changes I'd be making and asked if there was anywhere else we could store the garbage cans—according to my Bagua, they were affecting my fame and reputation.

They just turned around and left.

Great Moments in Digital History

If you've ever run a marathon, then you're probably familiar with how the grueling 26.2-mile event originated. According to myth, the race was originated by the Greek messenger, Pheidippides, the early version of FedEx. Dispatched from the front lines at the Battle of Marathon, Pheidippides ran non-stop to Athens, bursting into the assembly exclaiming, "Nenikékamen," or, "We have won" before collapsing and dying. Why didn't he just send a tweet?

The answer, of course, is that while he could have faxed or emailed the message to Athens, Twitter wasn't invented until hundreds of years later. If he *had* tweeted the message and skipped the run, chances are there wouldn't have been a Boston Marathon, the running craze of the 1970s, running sneakers or those cute little shorts we enjoy seeing on each others' heinies. Thousands of middle-aged, overweight couch potatoes would be even more middle-aged and overweight. There wouldn't have been much demand for sports bras and heaven forbid… there probably wouldn't be any Lycra.

History could have been completely re-written if our current technology was around when Moses approached the Pharaohs of Egypt prior to the great Exodus. Instead of threatening Egypt with swarms of locusts, turning the Nile into blood or killing off families' first born male children, he could have just shut down their Facebook accounts. The wailing would have echoed across the land. Or, he could have released a crippling virus into the Pharaoh's construction company's mainframe computer that would have resulted in building a deadly desert collection of million dollar hotels, wedding chapels, gambling casinos, golf courses, circus acts, computer-operated water fountains, amusement parks, brothels, shops and tourist traps in the middle of the desert.

The birth of Christ would have changed. Joseph and Mary could have avoided spending the night in a dirty barn with stinky animals if they had just jumped on Priceline.com with their iPhone app and checked out last minute hotel deals in Bethlehem. Chances are that Mary would have brought all her friends up to date with the following email:

Dear BFF:

Well, Joseph and I finally got here late last night. OMG! It took forever, riding on the back of that stupid donkey. We were supposed to be staying in the Emperor's Suite, but you-know-who screwed up our reservations. By the time we arrived, the only thing left was this dirty old barn behind the hotel. We were both so tired, we just said WTF and crashed in the hay. Then the argument. I told Joseph that I was pregnant and he completely lost it! I swore up and down that I didn't know how it happened. I've never slept with anyone—not even him. I insisted that it was Immaculate Conception, but he wasn't going for it. Not for one minute. He ended up stomping out and was gone for over two hours before he called me on his cell phone. He told me in order to cover the cost of feeding an extra mouth, he had to take a part-time job in the lumber department at Home Depot. A week after we got here, I gave birth to a 14 lb. baby boy. Holy #$%^. He barely fit in the manger. We're calling him Jesus (pronounced -HEY-SOOS). Later that evening, 3 wise men stopped by with frankincense, gold and myrrh. They got all bent out of shape when I told them that I had already received tons of frankincense and myrrh at my baby shower, but I'd go ahead and take the gold. They should have done a little research. I've been registered at the Crate N' Barrel in downtown Nazareth for days.

Monkey in a Pink Canoe

Well GF, that's about it for now. We should be back in a couple of months after Joseph makes enough dough for the trip back. We're hoping to upgrade to the back of a camel.

Mary

Christopher Columbus could have benefited enormously from today's technology. Anticipating the huge potential in capturing the spice trade of the East Indies, he set out in 1492 for Japan with financing from Queen Isabella of Spain. He ended up wandering aimlessly all over the western world: the Bahamas, the Greater and Lesser Antilles, the Caribbean, Central American and Venezuela. If he just had a GPS, Google Maps or Mapquest, he could have spared himself the embarrassment of not knowing where the @#$%^ he was and could have ultimately kept his job as the "Great Admiral of the Ocean." Instead, he was unceremoniously driven out of town with the rest of his family.

Long before the popular television series, "Noah's Ark," God became so upset with humankind that he decided do away with the lot of them, except for Noah and his family. If there had been electricity and telecommunications at the time, things would have been much easier. God could have just shut down the entire power grid to the world and watch everyone duke it out without their iPads. But there wasn't, so he decided to do the only thing he could: flood the earth and start over. Given simple power tools and a laptop with computer assisted drawing, it would have taken Noah a fraction of the 120 years it took to build an arc 300 cubits long and to maintain an inventory of two of every species. With Internet access, his sons could have completed an online degree in hotel management from the University of Phoenix while they bobbed along, waiting for the waters to recede—although it wouldn't have mattered. By the time they touched down on dry land, there wasn't anyone left to inhabit the earth, so reservations would have been down for a couple of hundred years.

It's safe to say that if technology had appeared earlier in history, hundreds of events would have changed. The Declaration of Independence would have had its own website and blog, the Wright brothers might have been the first TSA agents to do cavity searches at Kitty Hawk and there would have been no need for Gutenberg's movable type printing press. The first Bible would have probably shown up as a Blackberry app.

Shenandoahs, Pixie Cuts & Afrobobs

At the end of my haircut the other day, my barber asked, "Would you like me to touch up your eyebrows a bit?"

"I don't know," I said. I never really thought about it. "Do they need it?" The mere fact that he asked means that they probably did. People don't usually ask you, "Would you like some Listerine?" unless your breath is already peeling paint off the walls.

There was a time when no one would have asked me about my eyebrows. But, I guess that's one of the drawbacks of getting older. I also have to trim the inside of my ears, nose, my chest and have my back waxed. Some people have actually capitalized on their bushy brows—people like Andy Rooney, Susan Boyle, Peter Gallagher, Sam Waterston, Walter Cronkite, Martin Scorsese and Lt. Worf from Star Trek.

The entire way home, I ruminated over all of the people throughout history who have made fashion statements with their hair. You can bet Adolph Hitler's barber never suggested growing a handlebar moustache or mutton chops for a change. Nor would Wyatt Earp have been Wyatt Earp if he wore a little, one-inch moustache directly below his nose and his hair slathered across his forehead. Mr. T would never wear his hair like Donald Trump—and vice versa.

Because of the phenomenal strides made in hair transplants, I rarely miss an opportunity to ridicule anyone who wears a comb over—especially a really bad one. I don't know why a rich, high powered executive like David Gergen would want to spend hours in the morning stretching an 8-inch length of hair from one side of his head to the other when he could opt to have the entire top of his head riddled in hair plugs or covered with that spray paint for men. Besides, one stiff breeze and it kicks straight up like the lid on an open can of cat food. Then again, after serving as advisor to four U.S. Presidents, his lapse in tonsorial judgment obviously hasn't hurt his career. I just wish someone would tell him how ridiculous he looks. Why not just shave his head? Hey, it worked for Dwight Eisenhower and James Carville.

Once upon a time in medieval Japan, having a bald head with a ponytail was a mark of distinction and virility. Even if they had a full head of hair, ruthless Japanese Samurai would shave the tops of their heads and pull their ponytails back tighter than a banjo string. It was done to help keep their helmets on their heads, so it probably wouldn't work that well for David Gergen. I've never once seen him in a helmet.

Then, of course, there's the powdered wig. Kings, aristocrats, presidents, politicians and composers wore them throughout history. Present-day barristers in England still wear them. It all started with King Louis XIII of France. He suffered from male pattern baldness and was sick of being mocked by the King of England, so he wore the biggest wig he could find. By 1665, anyone with aspirations of moving up in European society wore one—the bigger the better—although I don't think it would catch on now. Despite television commercials to the contrary, you really can't swim or run on the beach wearing a powdered wig.

Men continue to express their individualism by wearing full beards, chinstraps, goatees, handlebar moustaches, neckbeards, Shenandoahs, sideburns, soul patches, two-day stubbles, toothbrush moustaches and Van Dykes. Both sexes continue to choose from a variety of hairstyles that have been around for decades: the afro, bob cut, bowl cut, bun, buzz cut, cornrows, crew cut, dreadlocks, duck's ass, finger wave, flattop, French twist, the jarhead, Jheri curl, Liberty spikes, Mohawk, mullet, pageboy, pigtails, pixie cut, pompadour, ponytail, shag, updo and waves—with and without bangs.

On the other hand, women battle hirsutism by shaving, tweezing, depilating or waxing unwanted hair from every nook and cranny of their bodies. They'll attack superfluous hair over their lips, underneath their arms, their sideburns, nipples, middle of their chest, belly buttons, beards, arms and legs. And then there's the pubic region. Even though no one's supposed to see it, women will let their pubic hair go au naturel or trim it into a triangle, landing strip (ironically, called a Hitler's Moustache), heart, diamond, spade and club, arrow, pyramid, freestyle, attach pubic hair extensions or do away with the entire growth with a Brazilian wax.

It wasn't until after I got home and did a little research, that I discovered how many ways there are to interpret "touching up my eyebrows a bit." Originally, I thought my barber just wanted to cut them with scissors. I found out later that had I said 'Yes', he might have started tweezing, waxing, restoring or threading. I don't have a unibrow, so he probably wasn't thinking of doing an eyebrow transplant. Nor do I think I need an eyebrow lift.

Besides preventing sweat, water and other debris from falling into your eye sockets, eyebrows are important in communication and facial expressions. It's hard to imagine Sean Connery being very sexy without eyebrows.

So, the next time someone asks you if you'd like your eyebrows "touched up a bit," pause before you answer. You may have no idea what you're getting yourself into.

Bwuck-Bwuck-Bwuck, Phltttttt

Late last night, I was yanked away from the season finale of "The Desperate Lives of Atlanta Housewives" by an urgent knock on the door. It was Ping. Ping recently emigrated from Thailand and is boning up for his citizenship examination by taking English lessons. Taking pity on anyone having to learn English as an adult, I graciously volunteered to help tutor him with the nuances they never teach you in language school.

"If you really want to fit into the fabric of American society," I told Ping, "You'll have to learn American slang and the thousands of grunts, hand signs, gestures and sounds we Americans use to take the place of the 500,000 proper English terms we've dropped since learning to speak our first words. Like the Check Please gesture.

The Check Please gesture originated in the U.S., but has rapidly spread to every corner of the globe. Effective from the smallest bodega to the ritziest eatery, the gesture is used when you're ready to leave and want the waiter to bring you your check—now. Start by thrusting your arm into the air and snapping your fingers repeatedly until you get their attention. Follow this by pretending to hold a writing implement and make a squiggly motion with your hand. Simple, but useful, the Check Please gesture has managed to erode centuries of respect and decorum, when people used to have enough class to wait patiently for their waiter to come by, inquire about the service and ask if they would care for anything else.

Ping mentioned that a cute girl in his class had caught his attention, but he was too shy to speak to her. No problem. I told him that American men never speak to women when flirting, anyway. Instead, it's customary to communicate your feelings by throwing her an Air Kiss. Since its inception, the Air Kiss has acquired several alternative interpretations. If Higginbottom from the Marketing Department throws you one during the sales presentation you just bungled, it's called the Kiss of Death and probably means you'll be looking for a new job before the day is out. On the other hand, if a 300 lb. biker thug in prison sends you an Air Kiss from the other side of the mess hall, it means that he (not you) is going to get lucky tonight—especially if he adds the Beckoning Sign—the palm held upward while repeatedly curling their index finger at you.

Hand gestures are indispensible when you'd like to publicly humiliate someone behind their back. To intimate to your boss that your office mate is a raging alcoholic and hits the sauce during work hours, make the Drinky-Drinky motion by forming a fist, sticking out your little finger straight and pretending to drink from your thumb. It's a great way to generate baseless rumors and get someone fired. Related to the Alcoholic gesture is the Stoner sign. Put your index finger together with the tip of your thumb, press them against your lips while you pucker up, sucking in air. Then point at the poor sap's back. He'll be gone by lunch.

A number of gestures are so complicated they require two hands—like the Bras d'honneur gesture. Originated in France (where else?) the Bras d'honneur gesture (also known as the Up Yours) is used to communicate extreme displeasure. Flex your arm while grabbing the inside of your elbow with the other hand in one smooth action. It's easy and works as effectively on police officers as it does your in-laws, landlord or judges handing down your fifth DUI sentence.

Air Quotes come in handy when the message absolutely, positively has to get there on time. You can use them in school, at the office and at home. Simply raise two fingers from each hand and hold them even with your eyes. While emphasizing specific words or phrases, crook your fingers twice. You might use it when you say to your girlfriend, "I thought we both agreed that we were going to have a *flexible relationship*."

If two hands aren't enough to get the message across, it's comforting to know that you still have other options—like creating gestures with other parts of your body. One of the most popular is the Bronx Cheer (also called blowing a raspberry). Meant to express derision, you can send someone a Bronx Cheer by sticking your tongue out and blowing until you produce a loud "Phlttttttttt." It's simple, effective and easy to hide in large groups.

When you want your roommate to be the first one to ski off a 200-foot cliff in unchartered mountainous terrain, goad him into action with the Chicken Gesture by placing your hands under your armpits and flapping your elbows up and down, while uttering, "bwuck-bwuck-bwuck." The Chicken Gesture is surprisingly effective at getting people to do things they normally wouldn't do in a million years—especially if their girlfriend is watching.

Other important gestures to learn are the Choking Sign, Rolling your Eyeballs, Blah-blah-blah, Pulling the Trigger, Shrugging, Making the Sign of the Cross, Slashing Your Throat and Mooning. All are easy to learn and surprisingly effective when words just won't do.

After two hours of practice, I could see that Ping was beginning to fade, so we wrapped up our session for the evening. But, even the late hour couldn't extinguish Ping's enthusiasm for his newly acquired language skills. "I can't wait until the swearing in ceremony next month," said Ping. "I'm going to Moon the Magistrate, send her a Bronx Cheer and walk around the room like a chicken!"

Paws for Prisoners

I found Bailey when he was an endearing pup at the Kansas City SPCA. I was looking for a dog to fill the void after Tucker died and couldn't afford a Tibetan Mastiff, Pharaoh Hound or King Charles Spaniel.

After a couple of years, Bailey blossomed into a full-fledged member of our family. He cared for the kids, frolicked in the swimming pool and went after squirrels brave enough to venture into our back yard. He was always eager to shoulder his share of the load by taking out the trash and doing the laundry and he even enjoyed a seat at our dinner table. He even cleaned up after himself when he did his duty on the back lawn. By the time he was 3, he surprised even his piano teacher by learning how to read Mandarin, Punjabi and Min Bei and started tutoring all the kids in the neighborhood. He was such an affable, talented canine I started looking for ways to share his talents with the rest of the community.

I first saw the advertisement for *Paws for Prisoners* while riding the bus to work. It boasted that the Paws program was a collective effort between advocate groups, local animal shelters and Leavenworth Federal Penitentiary where the inmates taught dogs basic obedience and shared mutual social skills. In return, the animals provided companionship to incarcerated felons. I don't know why they felt convicted felons were in a position to teach dogs obedience and social skills. After all, wasn't it the absence of social behavior that got them there in the first place? But, what the heck? Maybe he'd learn something new.

I drove Bailey to the Leavenworth induction center at the crack of dawn on Monday morning. As part of the arrangement, I agree to commit him to the program for a minimum of six months. That meant short of visiting days, this would be the last time I'd be able to pet him for a while. Neither one of us could anticipate the changes he was about to experience.

The Canine Unit took charge of Bailey, where they stripped him of his personal collar, took away his toys and de-loused him. This was followed by an extensive cavity search for contraband and a formal introduction into the Federal Penal System. As I turned to leave, Bailey looked at me with a stare that was a combination of anxiety and anticipation, as he pissed on the guard's foot.

The next morning, Bailey was assigned to his inmate handler. Whitey "The Weasel" Bauman was the leader of the Aryan Brotherhood, doing 10 consecutive life sentences for armed robbery and operating a motor vehicle with an expired learner's permit. Because Bailey was a German Shepherd, the program officials thought he and Whitey might be a good fit. Personally, I was relieved to hear the news. Everything I've read about prison life said it's impossible to survive if you're not a member of a gang, so I'm glad Whitey took Bailey under his wing.

Bailey wasn't allowed to communicate with the outside world for the first two weeks of his incarceration. The prison officials knew from experience that the key to successfully surviving life in the pen was to sequester new inmates from the outside world, giving them an opportunity to completely assimilate their new environment. Whitey kept him busy. He showed him how to change the sheets on his bunk, where to sit in the mess hall, how to carve a shiv out of a Milk Bone and introduced him to some of the other Aryan dogs in the yard.

Monkey in a Pink Canoe

My first opportunity to visit Bailey came three weeks later. As he shuffled into the visitor's room under shackled paws, I nearly fainted when I saw he had shaved his head. Tattooed around his neck was "Dog Pride World Wide" and "Skin Head" across his knuckles—well, whatever dogs have in the place of knuckles. When I slid a new Frisbee through the visitor's screen, he gave me a look of pity—like, "What a pathetic attempt to make up for my hollow childhood." He was copping quite an attitude.

The other thing that disturbed me was he started smoking again. He said everyone smoked in prison—even the cats. Cigarettes are the universal form of barter, so I promised to bring him a couple of cartons and some doggy porn on my next visit. "It's tough wedging a cigarette in between my toes," he said. "And try firing up a disposable lighter without opposing thumbs. It's virtually impossible." He thought about switching to smokeless tobacco, but there's nothing more disgusting than spitting all over your cell— even for a dog.

It was apparent to me after several more visits, what seemed like an opportunity for Bailey to make an altruistic contribution to the world was having the reverse effect on him. Instead of helping Whitey curtail his violent tendencies, Bailey was slipping into a pattern of anti-social behavior himself and spending more and more time in solitary confinement. He refused to respond to simple commands like, "Sit, stay, down, heel and fetch." Instead, he was picking up new ones like "Play dead" during knife fights, "Piss on the warden" and "Crap" when Whitey wanted him to poop out the contraband the other inmates' wives pushed up his rectum during visiting hours. Small condoms filled with drugs were one thing, but smuggling cell phones, Buck knives and 9mm handguns was really starting to take its toll on Bailey.

It was clear to both of us Bailey wasn't going to be able to fulfill his 6-month obligation with the Paws program, so we started making plans to bust him out of there. Well, not escape from prison, but rather through negotiations with the warden for an early release. By that time, Whitey was spending most of his time in the hole anyway, so Bailey wasn't offering him much companionship. That worked in his favor. On the other hand, Bailey had become a popular member of the Aryan smuggling operation, so they were reluctant to let him go until his contract was up.

We finally hired a lawyer: Berman Mendenhall from San Francisco. Mendenhall had experience with terminating contracts between animals and the Department of Justice. He was able to free Bailey on a technicality. Since he couldn't speak or sign documents himself, Bailey's contract was legally null and void. He was free to go.

I picked up Bailey outside the Leavenworth gates at ten o'clock on a Friday morning and drove him to his halfway house where we met his parole officer. Even though he hadn't committed any crimes, the DOJ felt is was in Bailey's best interests if he eased back into society slowly. After all, there were a lot of new things that he'd have to adjust to since he was incarcerated: having to pick up his own poop again, bark-control collars and Skype dog bowls. Not to mention he'd have to learn how to drive. I wasn't going to schlep him across town three times a week for his drug tests.

When I heard Leavenworth was terminating the Paws for Prisoners program, I had mixed feelings. While I was glad Bailey had a chance to do something nice for the inmates, I was relieved that I had the old Bailey back. Once his hair grows out and we have his tattoos removed, he'll be as good as new.

Betty Crocker Means Good Nutrition

As a rambunctious kid growing up in southern California, I was lucky enough to live at home under the loving dictatorship of two middle-income parents. In exchange for a few menial tasks like mowing the lawn, pulling weeds and cleaning out the septic tank, my parents gave me a comfortable place to live, a weekly allowance and home-cooked meals.

After I joined the Navy, it still didn't dawn on me that I couldn't cook. Why would it? Every day at five o'clock, we sauntered over to the mess hall, grabbed a dented aluminum tray, a knife and spork and stood in line for whatever slop they were pushing on us. We spent the rest of the evening debating over exactly what it was that we just ate and what it was likely to do to us. But at least I didn't have to prepare it.

It wasn't until several years later that I had to figure out how to feed myself. By the end of my tour of military duty, I was too old to go back home and couldn't afford a personal chef, so I was on my own. I'd either have to get married, learn how to cook or wither away to nothing.

As a young bachelor, it didn't take long to discover that there were several options for feeding myself. The first was eating out. If you don't care about good nutrition, cholesterol, sodium content, calories or price, you can find anything you want by going out to eat. For a few bucks more, you can order in. You never have to leave the comfort of your couch or change out of your stained sweatpants to stay well fed.

I started with the cheapest, greasiest fast food joints I could find. Howard Johnson's, Shakey's Pizza, Kentucky Fried Chicken, McDonald's and Bob's Big Boy were minutes away from my apartment, so I knew I'd be alright. I might die of Rickets, Beriberi, Pellagra or Scurvy, but I'd never starve. The joints with drive-thru windows got most of my business.

By accident, my roommate and I found Friggenberg's Swedish Smorgasbord. For $5.95, we discovered a foolproof way to eat for days. We'd walk up to the cashier and ask for a take out tin—one of those round aluminum pans with the cardboard tops. We never had any use for the tops, so we used them as disposable Frisbees.

The structures we built violated the local building codes for maximum allowed height. We'd start by spreading a layer of mashed potatoes over the bottom and sides of the pan. This was our foundation and helped to anchor everything else in place. You can use herring salad or refried beans, but we found that mashed potatoes were more adhesive, better weight bearing and nearly bullet-proof after being refrigerated. Then, we'd press carrot sticks vertically into the mashed potatoes around the circumference of the pan. This provided a six-inch high framework and supported everything that was to follow. After lining the inside of the carrot sticks with a layer of cabbage leaves, we were ready to start filling our masterpiece. We'd add the heaviest first—Swedish meatballs, sliced meats, various cheeses, sausages, cabbage rolls and Lutefisk followed by a variety of salads, rice pudding and jello, covered by a thick layer of gravy for the ride home. If it was raining, we'd cover the structure with an upside down tostada shell. The result was a 15-pound take-out pan that took two of us to carry out to the car. We were set for days.

Eventually, I got tired of eating out every night and because of my unusual table manners, I didn't receive many invitations for dinner, so I moved into the "box" phase.

Betty Crocker made a wide variety of bachelor cuisine—the most popular was Hamburger Helper. It came packaged as Bacon Cheeseburger, Cheese Lover's Lasagna, Cheesy Enchilada, Cheesy Beef Taco, Cheeseburger Macaroni and Cheesy Pasta and Broccoli-Cheese Hamburger Helpers. Fortunately, I liked cheese because that seemed to be the central ingredient in every one of them. Just add a pound of ground beef, stir it together and you have all the essential food groups in one pan. For a change of pace, I'd exchange the hamburger with Spam, canned shrimp, tuna, pork, chicken or canned cocktail weenies. When I was out of everything else I'd steal one of the dog's Alpos.

After I got bored with Hamburger Helper every night, I moved on to the frozen food phase: TV dinners, Banquet fried chicken dinners, Swanson's Hungry Man, Chinese food and frozen vegetables. The weight I gained was a natural segue to Healthy Choice, Lean Cuisine and the Weight Watchers, which ultimately eroded to mixing Slim Fast with beer. Then I discovered the magic of the crockpot.

Large and indestructible, you can throw almost anything into a crockpot and come away with something that's at least marginally edible. My crockpot came with a small cookbook, so I went ahead and tossed it in. I'd usually start with some type of animal part: an unidentifiable slab of meat, cut up chicken or whole cow's tongue, then covered it with a can of some sort of liquid and anything I could find from the back of the refrigerator that's wasn't already green. That was it. Whatever resulted usually wasn't too bad by the time it simmered for 18 hours. There were only a few times when the smell drove us out of the apartment. Most of the time it made enough to feed me and all of my roommates for a week, so I only had to cook once—if you call pressing the ON switch cooking.

It wasn't until much later that I started experimenting with the strange substances known as vegetables. As a child, I vaguely remember watching my mother chopping up plants for dinner, but I was clueless as to what she did with them. I should have paid better attention. It's hard to cook with vegetables. They all have their own personalities and if you overcook them, you'll end up with a large pot of something that vaguely resembles the New York Times left out on the driveway in the rain. Fortunately, I didn't have to wait long for the next phase: the gas grill.

You'll find a gas grill on every deck across the United States. They're easy to use, too. When you get home from work, just fire up the grill and throw on anything of animal or plant origin until it's black, and voila! It's mealtime. The best part is there are no dishes to clean. When I'm really lazy, I'll stand in front of it and eat right off the grill.

I don't know how I've survived all these years with my unique approach to nutrition. But, the fact that I've lived to be as old and fat as I am attests that I must have done something right. I can hardly wait to see what they come out with next that makes cooking even easier than the microwave. When it does, I'm in.

I Don't Feel as Good as I Look

When I was younger, I was indestructible. Or, at least I thought I was. All through my teens and twenties, I would routinely risk life and limb, cliff diving in Acapulco and driving at the speed of sound the wrong direction up one-way streets—all without a thought to the consequences if something were to go wrong. Old age has changed all that.

Nowadays, before I even open my eyes in the morning, I run through a comprehensive physical checklist prior to swinging my feet out of bed—lower back: check. Right and left knees: check. Feet and ankles: check. Hands, wrists and elbows: check. Head and neck: check. If my inventory passes muster, I'll pad into the kitchen to make coffee. If it doesn't, I'll initiate a whirlwind of events, ultimately leading to my funeral.

My last episode began with an innocuous pain on the inside of my cheek. Most people would consider it a minor inconvenience, then get on with their day. Not me. I need to know exactly what's wrong with me and how it's going to impact the rest of my life. Could this be the beginning of what eventually takes me down?

By running the tip of my tongue over the affected area, I began to manufacture enough symptoms to warrant researching the malady on WebMD. I'm not usually interested in what the discomfort *is*, but rather what it could be. WebMD has a handy symptom checker that lets me catalogue all of my daily aches and pains, saving them in a personal online profile on Facebook and Twitter. If anyone asks, "How are you today?" I can give them more information than they probably want.

Next, I clicked on the site's body map. After zeroing in on the face (they didn't ask if it was inside or outside), they presented a number of symptoms such as memory loss, drooping of one side of the face, uncontrolled flatulence, visible deformity, constipation, impotence as well as 20 others. The worst one I could find that fit the bill was mild pain and discomfort. Then I had to choose if it was dull or achy, burning or stinging, throbbing or none of the above. Since it was so early in the diagnostic process, I chose the latter.

After additional refinement of my symptoms, it ultimately suggested some possible diagnoses: trigeminal neuralgia, osteomyelitis, fractured eye socket, leprosy, salivary duct abscess, three types of cancer and a number of other lesser problems like sinusitis or toothache. But, I immediately ruled all of those out as too simple.

After some additional probing with a pair of French fry tongs, I decided to settle on trigeminal neuralgia. It had a nice ring to it and would sound good in my obituary. It also had the most potential for gathering sympathy and getting prescriptions for powerful painkillers and sedatives.

Now that I knew what the pain was, I needed to start planning how my TN was going to impact the rest of my life. Nothing I read said anything about how long I could expect to live with this life-threatening condition, so I decided to assume the worst—I only had a few months to live. That being the case, I started to get my house in order.

I went into Microsoft Outlook and generated a new email distribution group—"Friends to Receive Death Announcements." That way, I could mass email the bad news to all of the people who still owed me money while I moved on to other important tasks. Since

I wasn't entirely sure how long I had to live, I thought I'd better get a haircut. It makes it so much easier for the mortician should you suddenly drop dead. And, given that it was likely to be a closed casket service, I cancelled my gym membership—no sense worrying about losing weight anymore. I also sold my car, skis, golf clubs, furniture and gave away all of my clothes except for one nice suit and a few hospital gowns I had left over from my last knee surgery. They could come in handy should I become bedridden toward the end.

I continued by cancelling my memberships to Dateafelon.com, REI, Jenny Craig, the Cheese of the Month Club, The National Rifle Association and submitted my three month notice for termination of service for my utilities, Internet access, cell phone service and NetFlix. Even if I ended up hanging around longer than I intended, they sometimes offer terminal patients discounts in their final hours, so it was worth the risk.

The next day, my symptoms actually started to subside a bit, so I used the end of a ball peen hammer to press against the side of my cheek until they returned. I found if I pressed hard enough, I could even cause some wicked discoloration which would look horrendous and confuse the dickens out of the Medical Examiner during my autopsy.

Over the next month, I struggled with my TN; no matter what I did, it seemed to get better. So, I started chewing beer cans and sleeping with a rolled up sock inside my mouth to try to recoup my symptoms. Unfortunately, no matter what I did, the pain began to subside. By the end of the week it was completely gone.

It's been a while since I've woken up with any new complaints. That's OK. I lost my job, and with it my medical insurance, so I'll need to curtail all my visits to the doctor and the dozens of prescription medications that line my nightstand. But I do have more free time to spend on WebMD now. In fact, I think I feel a new lump on the back of my neck...

Space-Aged, High-Capacity Sports Bras

While rummaging through my old junk drawer, I came across one of my prize possessions: a ballpoint pen that writes upside down and was endorsed by NASA. In 1965, it was the must-have accessory of the times. Not only could you use it to write letters while lying in bed, you could draft a note in zero gravity, on greasy paper in a wide variety of temperatures—all while submerged underwater.

For the life of me, I can't think of a single instance when I've cursed to myself, "Dang, I wish I had a pen that wrote upside down, underwater and on greasy paper." But, it probably would come in handy if I was ever buried alive in a coffin or needed to scribble a note to my editor explaining that this week's column would be late because I just drove off a bridge and was presently lying underwater at the bottom of a lake.

Since that time, clever marketing pros have come up with thousands of ways to enrich the quality of every day products. In 1974, the suave actor Ricardo Montalban became famous for pitching the 1974 Chrysler Cordoba with soft, Corinthian leather. It's a mystery how the tiny Greek city got caught up in supplying upholstery to over-priced, American sedans, when if fact, the seats were actually covered with American cowhide and vinyl products from a plant outside of Newark, New Jersey. But, it worked.

There's no end to the list of products that have been enhanced with carefully selected buzz words used to increase their perceived value or versatility. Any product that is Space Aged will undoubtedly be better than one that isn't—particularly if it's made from titanium or carbon fiber and was used by astronauts on the Space Shuttle. Whether it's Tang, electronics, insulation, underwear, plastic, zit cream, shampoo, suppositories, LED lights or toilet paper, if it spent time in space, it must be good.

Products that use Advanced Technology are so far ahead of their time, we probably don't appreciate them. Touch Screen, digital, Bluetooth and high definition rectal thermometers *have* to be better than the glass and mercury models used since the 1600s. Even though they all do the same thing, it's comforting to know that you're being probed using the very best that technology has to offer.

Any products or services with Fast, EZ, 3-minute or Xpress preceding their names will always outsell more accurate, hand-made or personalized items. Consumers want it fast and they want it now. We'll always drive through fast food joints, dry cleaners, pharmacies, video outlets, gas stations, doctor and dentist offices, grocery stores—even outpatient surgical centers and synagogues—if it means we don't have to get out of our cars.

Some products are guaranteed winners—anything to do with enhancing your abs, tightening your butt, enlarging your breasts, covering gray hair, removing unwanted hair, losing weight or eliminating the necessity to cook. But you have to be selective when choosing the appropriate marketing terms. High capacity may be an appropriate term to use for backpacks, washing machines and gas tanks but you probably don't want to use it with diapers, condoms, jock straps, sport bras or airsickness bags. Sticky and See-through are great features for office supplies but not for women's clothing. On the other hand, just about any consumer product can benefit from being holistic, artisanal, lightweight, odor-free, high-fiber, one-touch, organic, gluten-free, latex-free or zero-calorie.

Another clever approach Madison Avenue has tried to sell goods is by attaching "O-Matic" to the end of products or service names. Sling-O-Matics, Rinse-O-Matics, Flex-O-Matics, Ice-O-Matics, Wax-O-Matics, Slice-O-Matics, Select-O-Matics, Stack-O-Matics and Tune-O-Matics have sold millions on their name value, alone. On the other hand, you're not likely to see many Vasectomy-O-Matics, Lasik-O-Matics, Birth-O-Matics, Colonoscopy-O-Matics or Divorce-O-Matics.

The popularity of the Information Super-highway has made it much easier to reach out to consumers with alluring product names. Let's face it—everyone has a Facebook page, Twitter account and RSS Feed that are pummeled by hundreds of ads for hemorrhoid creams, Viagra, walkers, porn sites, electric scooters and telephones with buttons the size of Wheat-thins.

It's been quite a while since I've needed to write a letter upside down and under water, but just in case I do, I make sure I'm never far from my space-aged, titanium, high capacity, NASA endorsed astronaut's pen. It's not likely that a product so suited to the American consumer will ever come my way again.

The Benefits of Benefits

Bert let me have all the ice cream I could eat. He was that kind of boss. He also knew I was likely to be the only white 15-year-old boy that would be dumb enough to agree to drive his ice cream cart through East L.A. in the middle of summer. The free ice cream was compensation for having to listen to 5 uninterrupted hours of Brahms's Lullaby while being robbed at gunpoint.

Mention the word benefits and the first thing people think about are medical, dental, vision, paid vacation, sick leave and a 401(k) plan. Unbeknownst to employees, they're designed to keep your body up and running, because when it comes right down to it, a healthy body is an overworked body. Overweight, stressed-out sales managers don't contribute much to the bottom line when they're succumbing to a heart attack in mid-flight from L.A. to Cleveland on Christmas Eve. Gone are the days of "touchy feely" benefits like free lunches at the company cafeteria, passes to Disneyland and Bring Your Mother-in-Law to Work Day—always one of my favorites.

So, last year after being hired for what appeared on the surface to be a great opportunity, I decided to look closely into my benefits package. What immediately caught my attention was that my benefits didn't kick in until 90 days after I was hired. Since they were basically saying I was worth LESS for the first 89 days of employment, I made a conscious decision to slack off until the end of the third month.

One of the other things I was grateful for was their first-rate Employee Assistance Program. Based on the excessive employee turnover and the screams coming from the window ledges, I anticipated becoming a hopeless alcoholic and getting pathetically hooked on prescription painkillers inside the first 6 months. I was relieved to hear that they offered a quality rehabilitation program. A 28-day stint at the Betty Ford Clinic would be my little Christmas present to myself.

In Section Two of the employee handbook, Critical Illness and Accident plans were explained. While I've always been a healthy man who tries to watch what he eats, exercises and gets regular check-ups, it was comforting to know that I was of more value after, rather than before a massive heart attack or going blind. Each event potentially paid thousands of dollars, so if I planned them carefully, I might be able to suffer from kidney failure while simultaneously having a heart attack and stroke while I was under a coma. By the time I came to, I'd have thousands in the bank while the company figured out what to do with me, now that I couldn't speak, see out of my left eye and was restricted to the use of my non-dominant hand to write childlike messages on a blackboard. They'd find something to do with my functioning feet.

The benefit plan went on to describe in gory detail the extent of some of its other coverage: you never want to get 3rd degree burns over just 35% of your body—always shoot for at least 36%—you get six times the benefits. Which means if your neighbor's house is burning to the ground and you've already saved their cat, run back in and look for grandma, the parakeet and all of their hamsters. Make sure you're extra crispy before abandoning your rescue efforts. The same thing goes for factures. Whenever possible, shoot for open, compound fractures instead of their wimpy hairline counterparts—you get a much higher return on your investment. Suck it up. You can handle a little more pain. You're going to be writhing in agony once they take you off the morphine drip anyway, so you might as well be well compensated.

Another thing that intrigued me is how insurance companies put a value on loss of limbs. According to my benefits manual, the loss of a single finger is only worth $750—hardly worth whatever it was that I was doing—while two or more losses could get me $1500. They don't specifically break the compensation down for an entire dominant hand, single opposing thumb or loss of an index finger (so critical in daily activities like picking your nose), so I make it a point never to shove my entire right hand into the photocopier. I'll always start with the little finger on my left hand. I've known dozens of people who have survived without three or four fingers on their left hand, but take away your right middle finger and you've lost virtually all of your communication skills when driving.

Since I'm so broke, I decided to carefully craft a major workplace accident that would result in the loss of my left hand, my right foot and one of my eyes—I haven't decided which one yet. I could make an additional $100,000 each for losing my hearing, speech or urinary continence. After I recover, they can find a spot for me visiting college campuses, interviewing new graduates.

If I can't make enough money through blatant bodily injury, I might be able to claim short-term disability or STD (not to be confused with sexually transmitted diseases) or long-term disability or LTD (not to be confused with Flowers LTD). Granted, I'd make less money, but I'd still be able to feed myself without having to have the night nurse chew my food for me and I could finally dispense with all of the catheters. If that wasn't enough, I could always take my Paid Time Off.

Paid Time Off (also called PTO) is accrued beginning the first day of work at a rate of .06543487935658472532113 per hour, while on assignment anywhere south of the equator during leap years. Other benefits include Extra Time Off, Unpaid Time Off, Sick Pay, Terminated Time Off and Incarceration Time Off. I could also elect to take a Leave of Absence for special family events like my 16-year-old daughter's marriage to the president of the Oakland Hell's Angels.

If having a job with great benefits still doesn't resolve my personal issues, I could always quit, collect unemployment, file a claim for Post Traumatic Stress Disorder and spend the rest of my pathetic life on the dole from the Federal government by living in a Veteran's Administration Psychiatric Hospital, making wallets and slippers. Or, by driving a three-wheeled ice-cream cart in the summertime.

The Happiest Peak on Earth

By the time the kids were let out for summer vacation, the climbing window for summiting Mt. Everest had already come and gone. I promised Shimmel that I would take him and his 8-year-old sister Toiba to the top of Mt. Everest as soon as his circumcision healed, but none of the guide companies would have anything to do with a middle-aged, sedentary writer and his two irascible children. So, we shifted gears and made plans to climb The Happiest Peak on Earth—the Matterhorn. Not the legendary mountain that dwarfs Zermatt, but the steel and cement behemoth located in the middle of Disneyland.

At 147-feet, the Matterhorn towers high over the violent border between Tomorrowland and Fantasyland. It's riddled with dangerous roller coaster cars, screaming kids, spilled soda and sticky cotton candy. Since opening in 1959, hundreds of climbers have plunged to their deaths after underestimating the complexity of the Matterhorn's North Face—the only route yet unchallenged. That's where we were headed.

Being so late in the season, we had trouble securing a spot at base camp. The only thing left was a small site in Pixie Hollow along with Tinker Bell and her fairy friends. While better than having to spend the night inside Sleeping Beauty's Castle, it meant we'd lose valuable time, backtracking to the Gibson Girl Ice Cream Parlor on Main Street for our supplies before beginning our ascent.

We met up with our Sherpa on the Tomorrowland Terrace. Ichabod worked days on the Finding Nemo Submarine Voyage, but agreed to guide us to the summit of the Matterhorn at night just for the challenge of leading an out-of-shape cubicle dweller and two children to the top—that and 10,000 Rupees.

Getting to the top posed a number of risks. We were planning on a rapid ascent without supplemental oxygen, so there was always the chance that one of us would come down with hypoxia or cerebral edema once we got higher than 100 feet. There was also the Park Police who patrolled the mountain at night, looking for intruders. It wasn't going to be easy. If we were to successfully summit the Matterhorn, we'd have to leave Pixie Hollow no later than 6:00 PM.

Ascending the Matterhorn without supplemental oxygen meant that we'd be able to skip spending the night at Tinkerbell's Breakroom. Instead, we could scurry up Goofy's Revenge, paralleling the left Bobsled track. With the cars tucked away for the night, the only hazards we faced were the homeless people camped along the bottom of the mountain at night. Hundreds of Anaheim's down and out rummaged around the base of the Matterhorn in the evening, looking for French fries, candy and change—anything they could find that fell out of the cars earlier in the day.

On Wednesday night, we made our move. Ichabod darted over and under the Bobsled rails, slithering behind a series of manmade waterfalls. It was almost impossible to keep up with him—the wheels on my Samsonite kept getting caught on the edge of my garment bag. By 11:00 that evening, we had successfully made it to the halfway point, so we decided to take a break. While the men-folk passed around pizza, I sent Toiba back down to the car for more beer.

If we were to successfully reach the summit and get down before sunrise, we'd have to leave the top no later than 1:00 AM, which left the kids tired, cranky and complaining about the crampons I made them wear over their rubber flip flops. They perked back up when I reminded them of how hard they trained for the trip and that I hadn't given them their allowances yet.

As with Mt. Everest, the final 10-feet of the ascent was the toughest. We had to circumnavigate gaping holes left over from when the park abandoned the Skyway Tram in 1994. Dealing with the kids' tantrums on the way up left us only 15-minutes to savor the summit of the Matterhorn. We were on top of the world. Or at least pretty high up in Anaheim. We could make out the Mark Twain Riverboats, It's a Small World, the Santa Ana freeway (already backed up with morning commuters) and an Arby's on South Harbor Drive. Then it was time to hightail it back to the bottom before the lines to the ride started to form.

Most alpinists will tell you that the descent is always worse than the way up to the top. Our trip was no exception. Daylight had dawned and the lily-white skin peeking out of my Lederhosen was searing under the hot southern California sun. By the time I got to base camp, I had a nasty sunburn and doubted I'd be able to make it back to Splash Mountain, where the Park had scheduled an interview for us with Matt Lauer on the Today show. Apparently, we were the first family of three ever to scale the North Face of the Matterhorn without supplemental oxygen, during the middle of tourist season.

The interview ran late, exacerbating the most dangerous part of the journey—the Santa Ana Freeway back to LAX during rush hour in a rented Hyundai Accent. After being bumped off our flight 7 times and watching our gear fly off to Ohio, we finally made it home to Colorado to a crowd of excited well-wishers. The airlines promised our suitcases would be in Cleveland by morning. We could pick them up there.

The ascent to The Happiest Summit on Earth changed our lives forever. While none of us had to hike over frozen climbers who had given their lives to the mountain, the sheer length of the lines to the rides made us thank God that we were some of the fortunate ones—we'd be going home. Thousands of other tourists stuck in line wouldn't be so lucky. But, that's another story.

Those Good Old Time Diseases

I was a first-grader at Van Nuys Elementary School the first time I came into contact with the medical system. As a healthy child, the only thing that slowed me down was the occasional off-color weenie on "Hot Dog Friday." None of the hair-netted ladies behind the steam table thought for a minute that I could have something as serious as Ptomaine Poisoning and wouldn't have been able to recognize it even if I had. Instead, one of them took off her apron and marched me downstairs to the nurse's office where she laid me down on an old army cot that smelled of other 6-year-old kids.

Nurse Blumenthal looked like every other grammar school nurse—a clinical version of the Pillsbury Doughboy with a red cross centered squarely on the front of her hat. She was probably a cracker-jack clinician at some point in her career. But, you could sense that 30 years of working nights at the V.A. hospital had eroded her diagnostic skills to the point where she was grateful just to have a place to spend the twilight years of her vocation.

After feeling my forehead and poking around my mouth with a tongue depressor, she wrote off my symptoms as "being a kid."

Regardless of why I ended up in her office, Nurse Blumenthal always recommended the same treatment: a tablespoon of Castor Oil, a Mercury suppository and a note telling my mother I'd contracted a 24-hour case of Summer Complaint—also known as the backdoor trots, Montezuma's revenge or Tourista.

But I digress. Thanks to my parents' diligence, I managed to get through most of the common childhood diseases in a single year: Chickenpox, the Croup, Measles, Mumps, Whooping Cough, Cholera and Yellow Fever. Each malady was supposed to give me immunity against some other future disease—like the Shingles, 60 years later. Too bad nothing could have prevented my drooling and Alzheimer's.

It was all part of a carefully orchestrated plan. Instead of waiting for nature to take its course, my mother made me spend the night with every kid in the neighborhood who was flattened by Asperger's Syndrome, Diabetes, Rickets, Osgood-Schlatter Disease, Leprosy and ADD to improve my chance of getting them behind me before the Christmas holidays. Nowadays, kids are expected to succumb to a slew of newer, trendier diseases like Acne, Respiratory Syncytial Virus, Fifth Disease, Scarlet Fever, Impetigo, Kawasaki Disease and Reye's Syndrome. It's still too early to tell if exposure to any of those diseases will prevent them from coming down with the Collywobbles later in life. We'll just have to wait and see.

Up until the 1950s, diseases always had colorful names: Bilious Fever, Chin Cough, Crop Sickness, Dry Bellyache, Grocer's Itch and Bucket Fever that sounded far more serious than tendonitis, hay fever or influenza. According to my parents, half my family suffered from Lumbago or Consumption, while my great uncle Bert was leveled by Apoplexy. Two of my aunts passed away when their Grippe progressed to fatal Decrepitude. The rest succumbed to Dandy Fever, English Sweating Disease or Stupid Fever. One was hospitalized for months when her Milk Leg got the best of her after giving birth to a beautiful Mope-eyed girl. We never knew what any of those meant and neither did our doctors, but those were the medical terms they used. It was strangely comforting to know that our loved ones succumbed to something far more serious than merely slipping on a bar of soap.

We hardly see anyone with Black Water Fever anymore, although I'm sure it's still around. Penicillin, antisepsis and germ theory have eradicated most cases of Bad Blood, Bronze John and Jail Fever. But who's to say? I can't remember the last time I was quizzed on a medical history form, "Are you now, or have you ever suffered from Canine Madness, The Cooties, Dropsy, Dog Bark, Dancing Mania, Winterbottom's Sign, Softening of the Brain or Egyptian Inheritance?"

Certainly, standardizing the names of diseases and their treatment is one of the things that has driven up the cost of health care. Once upon a time, a simple case of Commotion was the same in Boston as it was in Twin Forks, Nebraska—and it was always treated at home with a week of bed rest followed by liberal doses of Winslow's Soothing Syrup (containing more than 65 mg of morphine). In fact, most cases of Noodlepox, Goiter and Philippine Itch were treated with Dr. Bonker's Celebrated Egyptian Oil, heroin tablets and Mack Mahon's Rattle Snake Oil Liniment. Patients struggling with obesity could look forward to a prescription for dehydrated tapeworms or their eggs.

It wasn't until later that people started running to physicians' offices for simple cases of Schistosomiasis, Scorbutic Fever and Scrumpox instead of patiently waiting for them to come to their homes. There, family physicians could better treat nasty cases of Frog Tongue, Nerve Pang and Scald Head with more sophisticated approaches like blood letting and applying leeches to suck out the bad body humours.

When patients complained of seizures, migraine headaches and depression, accommodating physicians began drilling holes in their heads (called Trepanation) to relieve pressure on the brain. And in 1936 a charismatic, innovative psychiatrist named Walter Freeman started performing Prefrontal Lobotomies without anesthesia by driving ice picks into his patients' eye sockets, then jamming them around in circles, "…cutting certain nerves in the brain, eliminating excess emotion and stabilizing the personality."

When health insurance started to be included as a standard job benefit, people immediately began abusing the medical system by running to the emergency room for things as simple as Catarrh, Shinbone Fever or Scrivener's Palsy. And, instead of treating their patients with proven, inexpensive compounds like cocaine throat lozenges, morphine sulphate, chloroform, codeine, heroin, powdered opium or cannabis indica, physicians drove up medical costs by ordering new fangled procedures like x-rays, biopsies, laboratory tests and magnetic resonance imaging.

To make matters worse, everyone has become a medical expert. Thanks to the Internet, Cosmopolitan, Good Housekeeping, Woman's World, Redbook and all of the other quality medical references in the checkout aisles, people now have a better understanding of their diseases and how to talk to their doctors. Gone are the days of simply accepting that their Mexican Trench Mouth is responding well to the blood letting. Today, every Tom, Dick and Harriet insists on learning exactly how he or she came down with Japanese Flood Fever, Sinking Chills or Sanguineous Crust. They want to know why after multiple electrical shock treatments, they're still hearing voices coming from the television.

Thankfully, we've grown into a kinder, gentler society when it comes to treating our medical complaints, even though it's caused the cost of medical treatments to continue to skyrocket. We no longer amputate gamey legs and psychiatrists stopped performing Lobotomies in 1967. But, pharmaceutical leeches do appear to making a comeback to help heal wounds and enhance circulation in narrowed veins. That is, once you've met your annual deductible.

Last Chance Undies

When I was a kid growing up in southern California, I'd try to escape the blistering summer heat by playing in the sprinklers on the front lawn or floating submerged in a public swimming pool until my fingers turned to prunes. I counted those hours under water as part of my daily hygienic practices. My mother didn't.

At that age I didn't know that the reason they chlorinated the water so heavily was because my classmates were peeing or Hershey squirting in the water. It looked clean to me. The way I looked at it, as long as I spent every day under water, I could go the entire summer without having to bathe. Since that time, I've learned a lot about good hygiene practices, but have committed to only a few. It's not that I have anything against being clean—I just have better things to do with my time than shower, wash my hair, brush my teeth and clean underneath my fingernails.

I wasn't interested in girls while in grammar school, so I wasn't particularly concerned about how I smelled. To be honest, I was completely oblivious to it. On occasion, I'd turn my T-shirts inside out to get a few more days wear out of them before they were destined for the laundry hamper. Walk into any 6th grade classroom and you'll get hit with the same smell: a pungent mixture of body odor, crayons and peanut butter sandwiches with a little bit of urine thrown in. It's called the smell of kids.

My father used to try to goad me into bathing regularly by regaling me with hygiene tales from his childhood. Being the youngest in a clan of eight, every Saturday night *his* father made him trudge barefoot through the snow to fetch buckets of clean water from the local creek. They'd heat the water on the stove, then pour it into the bathtub that sat prominently in the middle of the kitchen. Starting with his mother, each member of the family would bathe and wash their hair. By the time it was my father's turn the water was battleship gray and looked like a giant bowl of vegetable soup with a layer of soap scum and dead skin floating on the surface. Needless to say, he grew to appreciate a hot, daily shower.

According to the World Health Organization, more than 884 million people in the world have limited access to clean water. Even though Western countries do, we still persist in practicing some pretty odd hygiene habits. During the 1970s running craze, I remember reading an article by a Houston cardiologist who was a running guru and wrote for Runner's World Magazine. He insisted that there was a difference between nervous perspiration and good old-fashioned sweat. Perspiration was dirty. Sweat was clean. So, he would run to work every day and towel off before putting on his lab coat. Fortunately, he wasn't married and worked in a research lab so he didn't have to come into direct contact with many people.

Americans are unique in that most of us take a shower every day because we have plenty of water. Even in parts of Europe, taking a daily shower is considered extravagant. And, it's not likely you'll find kids in Bangladesh having water balloon fights or careening down Slip n' Slides into the Ganges river. Most of them still don't have indoor plumbing, so they sponge bathe like my father did. East Asian countries don't have toilets as we know them. Instead of commodes that allow you to sit while pinching a loaf, you have to squat in the catcher's position. Of course, that would never work in the United States. With more than half of the population being pathetically obese, they'd blow out their knees and have to be carted off to the hospital with their pants dangling around their ankles. On the other hand, we've developed a cottage industry for toilet seat risers and handles that lift you higher. It appears that we're moving in the opposite direction from the rest of the world.

Soft, absorbent toilet paper is also uniquely American. While visiting Munich one summer, the first thing I noticed was theirs must have been made out of recycled grocery bags. Instead of cleaning my brown-eyed Willy, it would just smear everything around. East Asian countries don't even use toilet paper. Instead, you'll find a bucket with a ladle sitting on the floor next to every squat toilet. After squeezing a steamer, people clean themselves with water, using their left hand to dry. That's why there are two things you'll never experience with Asian adults: 1) shaking their left hand and 2) skidmarks in their undies. Skidmarks are uniquely American and a constant reminder that we could be doing things better. The term doesn't even exist in the Vietnamese language.

Of course there are other hygiene practices to ponder besides keeping your alimentary exits clean. According to Dr. Oz, Oprah Winfrey's popular medical advisor, the average adult picks their nose 5 times a day. What they do with the result of these mining expeditions is anyone's guess. As a kid, I remember eating a few—but that was a long time ago. Still, they have to go somewhere. Look around. What's that hanging from the back of your sport coat? And, what about brushing your teeth, crop dusting, cactus legs and washing your hands after visiting the restroom? It's always baffled me why restrooms in restaurants have large, yellow stickers reminding employees that it's a federal offense to go back into the kitchen without washing their hands. I've personally never needed to be blackmailed with a felony to wash my hands after dropping a dookie. It just comes naturally. What I do have a problem with is electric dryers in place of paper towels.

We've all experienced it. You scrub up, rinse and look around for the towel dispenser. In its place is that impudent air drier. If I had noticed it before, I might *not* have washed my hands. With no other option besides drying your hands on the front of your shirt, you stand there, rubbing your hands together until they're red, chapped and bleeding. And, what do you do if you just washed your face? Inevitably, you'll squat down on all fours, pointing your face up into the jet stream until your hair stands on end or your mascara has melted half way across your face.

I'm not going to try to convince anyone that I have exceptional hygienic standards. There's still a little bit of the kid left in me that'll resort to a Pirate Bath or wearing last chance undies. Under exceptional circumstances, I've been known to take a Febreze shower or sniff the armpits of the shirt I want to wear. If the results are inconclusive, I'll douse them in English Leather. That'll usually get me by until I can convince myself that there's nothing wrong with wearing the same shirt for the rest of the week. Or, turning it inside out. Again.

The Mother of All Boredom

I'd been staring at the dime for over 20 minutes. After three-dozen attempts, I managed to balance it on edge and was struggling to move it across the counter top through a mishmash of telekinesis and sheer will power. I was bored.

I have no idea why the bank hired me in the first place. Besides having a pulse, I had virtually no marketable skills in the banking and finance industry. I didn't even *want* to work there. But, I did need the money and Elephant Butte Savings was the only place willing to give me a job, so I leapt at the opportunity.

It took me less than a week to discover the true meaning of tedium. Actually, it was closer to three days. Beside myself, there were 12 other bank tellers who sat staring into space from 8 to 5. Unlike our counterparts in the 1950s who actually worked for a living, we sat there nearly comatose, put out to pasture through a lethal combination of online banking, electronic deposits and ATMs. If I was lucky, a waitress might come in to personally deposit the $716 in loose change she'd collected as tips. And that was only because our ATMs wouldn't accept coins. After she left, I fidgeted on my hi-rise stool, searching for creative ways to make the time go by while keeping under the radar of management. If it weren't for all the robberies, it might have been a boring job.

We were forbidden to read in between customers, surf the Internet or talk on our cell phones. Those lent the air that we had nothing to do. Nevertheless, I was able to come up with a number of creative ways to entertain myself while appearing to be busy. I started by imagining that everyone who came into the bank was nude. Then I tried to see how long I could hold my breath without passing out. I gradually extended my record until the customers started complaining about the colors I was turning. After counting the number of hairs on my forearms, I'd push my index finger up my nose to see if I could touch my brain.

This wasn't the first time I'd been bored. My struggle with tedium went all the way back to when I was an infant lying in my crib. For the first six months, my only entertainment was making ca-ca in my Huggies. When I discovered that I could use the crap for finger painting on the walls, the world of free form art opened up to me—at least until the beatings started and my mother rolled the crib to the center of my room. Fortunately, by that time I had learned to crawl and pick my nose, so it was some time before I'd find myself bored again.

During college, I found temp agencies to be a low-stress, if boring, way to pay my tuition. Their expectations were even lower than mine, so it worked out perfectly. After counting ball bearings, collecting tolls and inspecting tortillas, I was convinced that temp agencies had the market cornered on low-paying, worthless jobs that never lead anywhere. But even good jobs have down time when there's nothing to do. You still need to *look* busy.

I found that as long as I had access to a computer I could look like I was embroiled in some high-level marketing analysis. By cradling the telephone receiver against my ear, I could convince anyone that I was up to my eyeballs in deadlines and final project approvals, so even my supervisors left me alone. It was even easier when telephone headsets came into vogue. There's no little red light that goes on like the outside of an occupied confessional, so my co-workers never really knew if I was talking on the telephone or just staring into space. The minute someone walked into my office and opened their mouth, I'd feign resignation and point to the headset as if to say, "Hey, I'd love to talk but I'm on the phone and this guy just won't shut up."

Later, I discovered I could fill hours just by walking down the hall glaring at a clipboard. People automatically assumed that I was swamped with work and barely had time to get to the restroom, let alone take the time to say hello. A friend of mine told me when he wanted to look busy he'd walk around with a bucket of paint and a paintbrush. After all, who would carry around a gallon of paint if they weren't in the middle of doing something important?

Of course, the mother of all boredom is the practical joke. You'll never find anyone gluing down the receiver of your phone or enveloping everything in your cubicle with aluminum foil if they're genuinely buried in work. The trick is to pull them off without your boss catching wind that you have nothing better to do with your time than to get back at your officemate by filling his drawers with packing peanuts.

Once I graduated from college and got my first management job, I thought my days of boredom would be over. Supervising a hundred employees should be enough to keep anyone busy—especially if they were as worthless as I was. What I achieved was a higher level of boredom. Even the president of the company confessed to me that he got bored. That's why they invented those expensive knickknacks called executive toys. Things like the Talking 8-ball, Panic Button or Tabletop Zen Garden Kit. I also had half a dozen miniature sports cars that I'd race around my pen and pencil set, pretending that I was a NASCAR champion on his final lap to victory.

Still looking for creative ways to defray my endless indifference, I happened upon a proven technique while watching reruns of "NYPD Blue." In the popular crime drama, Dennis Franz is always pissed off and jumps down everyone's throat. The technique works so well, it's been adopted by virtually every cop, medical and CSI show on television and the big screen. Beginning the next day, I started coming to work ticked off.

Finally, I found that I could combine all of the techniques for maximum effect. On any given day, I could instantly morph from my jovial self to a pissed off bank teller who was constantly yelling at someone on the phone while glaring at something on his clipboard.

After several weeks, the bank manager called me into his office to discuss my struggling performance. I knew I was in trouble, but considering all of the pencils he'd flipped into the ceiling tiles above his desk, I wasn't too worried about being called on the way I spent my time.

"Mr. Smith, we've had a number of complaints about your performance. The other tellers have complained that you appear to be under tremendous stress—yelling at the customers, excoriating people on the telephone and pacing the halls with a clipboard and a bucket of paint. For God's sake, man. You're just an entry-level teller. Maybe we expected too much from you."

He was right. I just couldn't deal with the stress of having nothing to do. So, we both agreed that the best place for me would be validating parking tickets in the basement parking garage. While I'd still be bored, at least I wouldn't have to pretend to be busy and I could continue working on my finger painting. Until I got bored again.

The Taco-Slinging Road-Kill Handler

It's that time of year again. When thousands of newly minted college graduates flood the workforce with their shiny new Bachelor degrees, heading for the first wrung on the ladder to the American Dream. But, unless you've already been recruited by a high-falutin' Wall Street investment firm, new college graduates will be faced with duking it out with all of their other classmates as well as thousands of military veterans and laid-off middle-managers who have been told to hit the pavement.

My first surprise came when I discovered that there was a paucity of good paying jobs for young people with Bachelor degrees in Comparative French Recreation. My guidance counselor talked me into the degree when I complained to him that all of the other classes were closed and I needed to graduate that semester. Nonetheless, he assured me that there would be thousands of reputable firms clamoring for bright stars who spent four years studying how to dress up in period costumes, juggling and painting each other's faces during Renaissance festivals. I pressed on knowing that if I was humble and willing to toil under a variety of adverse conditions to get my foot in the door, there's no end to where my education would take me.

When I started college, my parents agreed to pay for my tuition, room, board and car insurance—at least until I graduated. Once I left campus with my diploma in hand, I was on my own. But, I wasn't concerned. I knew that someone out there was clamoring for a bright, young man with my skills and all of those late nights working at The Big Taco would finally pay off.

The first job I landed was working as Cluckee the Chicken at Magic Mountain. While it wasn't exactly what I imagined, at least I'd be able draw upon part of my studies by dancing around in a bright yellow, 7-foot chicken costume (feathers and all) in 110-degree heat, passing out fliers to visitors as they entered the searing asphalt parking lot. Even though it was sweltering inside my chicken suit, it paid well and turned out to be an easy way to manage my weight. I could also ride the roller coasters as much as I wanted if I agreed to stay until after closing to help the attendants clean up all the puke from earlier in the day.

After the summer season ended, I started working in the criminal investigation field—as an apprentice for a crime scene clean-up crew. Sometime after the Law & Order and CSI boys left, it was my job to pick-up all of the body parts, remove the blood stains and scoop up the fluids that ran like a river through the living room. Initially, I thought since I'd be dressed in a yellow HazMat suit and cleaning up vomit, it would be a lot like working at Magic Mountain. It wasn't. Ultimately, I didn't feel that my college education prepared me for that type of work, so I asked to be transferred to another department within the company—the Road Kill department. For six months, I drove around southern California, covering every mountain road and truck stop looking for the unfortunate demise of inattentive wildlife that met the front bumpers of drivers caught by surprise. It wasn't much better than working a crime scene, but at least it was outside and they let me eat whatever I found on the side of the road.

During my road kill rounds, I would frequently drive by idle ski resorts preparing for their winter season. Images of snow bunnies in tight wool sweaters and stretch pants far outweighed the reality of shovels full of dead marmots and skunks, so I decided to pack my VW Bug and head for the high country. Winter was rapidly approaching and I knew that with my degree, I'd have no problem landing a job as an apprentice ski lift operator at Snow Summit in Big Bear Lake. In the beginning, working as a lift operator was oodles of fun. I got to spend every day outside shoveling snow off the chairlift seats and picking up overweight women who couldn't get up on their own—all in exchange for one free day of skiing a month.

Three months into the ski season, I was promoted to Supervisor of the mid-mountain unloading station on chair number one—most likely because of my academic achievements and the customer service techniques I demonstrated on the job. My task was simple—to insure that guests skied down the ramp safely, clearing the chair and on to the beginners' area. To offset the insidious boredom that inevitably crept into my day, I built a large ski jump at the bottom of the ramp, shaped like the Lost Pyramid of Giza—the same pyramid I studied in Freshman World History. As the skiers hit the jump, it launched them into the air at a forty-five degree angle, depositing them into two dog piles on either side of the ramp. It was loads of fun and supplied me with hours of entertainment, even though we'd occasionally send a beginner to the hospital. Evidently, one of them came back after their back surgery and complained to management. I thought for sure they'd reward my creativity with another raise and promotion, but instead, they banished me to the beginner's rope tow for the rest of the season.

When the ski area closed, I moved back home with my parents and once again, started my job search. I managed to find a series of challenging positions through one of the local Temp agencies. For the next six months, they sent me on an endless stream of two-week assignments at the Home Depot, Gas Depot, Lumber Depot, Plumbers Depot, Video Depot, Glass Depot, Office Depot, Depot Depot and every other type of do it yourself store that used college-educated, unskilled laborers—some with masters degrees and PhDs. Then it was off to another series of short-term assignments as a service station attendant, donut maker, taco slinger, dishwasher, ball bearing counter and a telemarketer for a cemetery. I liked cold-calling people at dinner time to discuss their immediate plans after death but eventually quit when I discovered how hard it was to generate repeat business.

After two years, I managed to find a bonafide career with a firm that was looking for someone with my credentials—someone who was young, college educated, impressionable, obedient and willing to work for less than $8 an hour—the same things employers are looking for today.

Interview with a Felon

Hi. I'm here for the job. I'm sorry I'm late, but I missed the last bus from the penitentiary because some of the other inmates started throwing food around at breakfast. By the time the guards gave us back our clothes and found all the hidden knives, I already missed my Thursday morning therapy session. Dr. Scheaselschwitz promised to write me a more powerful prescription so I can stop hyperventilating into brown paper bags before job interviews. But, it shouldn't be a problem with this one.

I read in the newspaper ad that you're looking for a mature, sharp-dressed, post-graduate educated CPA with extensive computer experience. Well, I don't have any of those skills but I'm a real fast learner. Just ask my cellmate. Besides, this place is only 5 minutes from the detention center, so I'd probably qualify for a work release program. My HOA meetings (Hostility Offenders Anonymous) are right on the way home, too.

I have a variety of valuable experiences. I'm sure you'll be able to find some of them useful at Fensterman's Fasteners. I grew up in the Nelbert B. Tubbs housing project and ran my own gang before I was 12, so I'm experienced in supervising different types of personalities. I'm also good at delegating work. For instance, one of The Mack-30 Daddies cheated me out of $50 and an 8-ball, so I told one of my homies to eliminate the problem. He did. As a reward, I gave him a nickel bag and let him spend the night with my little sister.

Evading the police has taught me how to think quickly on my feet, while developing unique solutions to everyday problems. Although my approaches to handling challenging situations might seem unorthodox to my co-workers, my parole officer encouraged me to apply for this job anyway. He said I've come a long way since the stabbings.

I'm a flexible team player and can work under stressful, adverse conditions. When I was a drug runner for the Latin Kings, four of us had to cram into a storm drain while the vice cops sicced their dogs after us. I'm also comfortable lifting heavy inanimate objects. Once, I came up with a way to stuff four Grape Street Crips into the trunk of a Toyota Corolla. Even the homicide detectives were impressed when they found them a month later.

I read at a 5th grade level, am fluent in ebonics and 17 other street-slang dialects, so if you have other people working here who used to be in gangs, I can translate for you. I also embezzled over $200K from the 42nd Street Locos so I know my way around financial records, Excel spreadsheets and Quicken. You might want to start me out in Accounting or Employee Payroll.

You're probably wondering about the tattoo on my neck. It's a python squeezing the life out of a puppy. I got it when I joined the Aryan Nation at Chino and have been meaning to get it removed as soon as I can find a job with health insurance. In the meantime, I can wear a turtleneck underneath my suit and tie, so no one will notice it unless they rip my shirt off during a fight in the lunchroom. Most of my other tattoos are on my back, chest, legs and around my genitals. The only way people will see them is if I have to roll up my shirtsleeves to beat the crap out of them. But that shouldn't happen very often once my reputation gets around the company.

You'll have to pardon the length of my hair, but I haven't been able to find a barber who's willing to work around lice. I used to wear

Monkey in a Pink Canoe

it shorter, but I grew it out to cover up the metal plate and staples I got from all the beatings in the yard. On special occasions, like when someone got paroled or made into one of the gangs, I'd have Fat Sylvester put it into cornrows. It looks real nice, and I didn't see anything about it in your Employee Handbook, so I might go with that. I'll also start shaving again as soon as the trustees let me have access to sharp objects, but I don't get that until I stop stealing from the new guys.

My psychiatrist suggested that I apply for a job that's away from other employees—at least for the first 6 or 7 months. I seem to work best in basements or other dark rooms with sensory deprivation, similar to solitary confinement. It should help cut down on my panic attacks until he can wean me off the Prozac, Xanax and Valium.

In answer to your question, "Why do I want to work here?" To be honest, I don't care where I work, as long as I can earn enough to cover my court costs and visit my old lady in Sybil Brand. She's due to be paroled September of 2075. I also need to support the 3 crack-babies we had while we were living together under the Vincent Thomas Bridge. That neo-natal intensive care gets expensive after a while.

Before we end for today, I need to ask you a few questions. First, how important are background investigations and polygraph results? Would you consider a couple of bad ones a deal breaker? I'm sure you'll agree that everyone makes mistakes and I wouldn't want to lose a perfectly good opportunity at Fensterman's Fasteners just because I exhibit violent tendencies or fail an occasional drug test.

What about my personal references? I have some, but you won't be getting much out of them because most of them are in lockdown or at the Norwalk State Mental Institution, where they don't allow the inpatients access to phones, paper or writing implements. The rest of them can't speak because of the feeding tubes. But we'll figure something out.

I've been looking at your company from the window of my cell for the past 15 years, dreaming of the day when I could come and work for you. I hope you're one of those people who believe that everyone deserves a second chance. Maybe even a third or a fourth. After my medications level off and I get this electronic ankle bracelet removed, I think you'll see that I bring a unique approach to everything I do. Thank you for letting me interview. You'll find a little something extra in this envelope.

Hoarding is the Life for Me

There was a time when I could move everything I owned in the back of my VW bug. Give me two hours and I could be on my way from a ski resort in northern California to picking pumpkins in Maine. All that's changed.

While no one has ever accused me of being a hoarder, I do find it hard to pass up a good deal when I find one. If I run across a special on melon-ballers, I never buy just one. I'll buy two. Or three. I never want to repeat the agony of having to dash out in the middle of the night searching for egg-yolk separators. The same thing goes for T-shirts, toothpaste, hemorrhoid cream, ballpoint pens, paper clips or Rosetta Stone Mandarin lessons.

My accumulating started during the Cold War of the 1960s. When things were looking particularly ominous, the Kennedy Administration urged all Americans to stock their bomb shelters with enough food to feed a family of four for a month. Our home didn't have a bomb shelter, so my dad retrofitted the hallway leading from my bedroom to the bathroom by throwing out all of my grandparents' wedding china, our best silver settings and 20 years of Christmas ornaments to make room for cases of every kind of canned goods known to man. We had enough Spam, canned weenies, fruit cocktail, bottled water and flashlight batteries to last us a lifetime. I still have some of those Saltine crackers in the back of my pantry and the Cold War has been over for more than 50 years. I just can't bear to part with them.

According to experts, hoarding is a "pattern of behavior that is characterized by the excessive acquisition and inability or unwillingness to discard large quantities of objects that would seemingly qualify as useless or without value." That's a nice way of saying you're a pack rat. But, in all fairness, it's easy to get caught up in hoarding. I, more than anyone, recognize how easy it is to get suckered into buying 50-pounds of hot wings at Costco because they're such a good deal. That's why I don't go there anymore.

It's almost impossible to differentiate pathological hoarding from plain, old collecting. As long as I can remember, my grandfather tried to get me started collecting coins. A true numismatic, he had volumes of rare coins that dated back to the civil war. Every year on my birthday, he'd beam as he presented me with a rare coin to add to my collection, in hopes that I'd follow in his footsteps. But, it never worked. I'd always end up busting out a priceless Liberty Head Nickel or 1933 Double Eagle to buy beer or cigarettes.

Some people have managed to blur the line between hoarding and collecting. Graham Parker is famous for his catalogued collection of navel lint, dating from 1964 to the present. Phil Miller has even created a term for himself—he's a Sucrologist—by collecting sugar packets from all over the world. But, nobody can compete with Debra Conant's collection of burnt food or Len Foley's array of old McDonald's burgers dating back to 1989. When I was in college, I collected empty beer bottles from around the world and creatively lined them up along all of the windowsills in our apartment. I thought they added a classy, international touch to the place and gave off a nice colored hue when the light was right. I also used to save all the pull-tabs from my beer cans. By folding them over themselves, I discovered that I could make inexpensive curtains to hang in the doorways.

Monkey in a Pink Canoe

People hoard all sorts of things—newspapers, TV Guides, take-out menus from Chinese restaurants and coupons to stores that went out of business 20 years ago. Some people even hoard animals. Every few years, you'll hear about an old lady who has died, leaving behind 45 cats, 23 dogs, 15 iguanas and cages of rats, bugs and other living things. Hoarding has gotten so bad that experts have come up with new terms associated with the pathology—like Goat Trails. A Goat Trail is a narrow path that winds around through canyons of old newspapers, discarded food or mounds of trash. Fortunately, my apartment hasn't gotten quite that bad. You can still see the carpet.

The worst things that I've accumulated are possessions that have no rational purpose. I have boxes of prescription medicines that date back to 1973. I have no idea what they do or what they were originally prescribed for, but if they were important enough to spend $20 then, they might come in handy sometime in the future—even if I won't know if I'm supposed to stick it in my eye, rub it over my elbow or push it up my bum. And, I can't call the doctor who prescribed them because he's been dead for 30 years.

I've managed to justify hanging onto clothes that I haven't worn since the Nixon era—the first one. While it's unlikely that I'll ever return to size 28-waist, vertical-striped bell bottoms, you never can tell. I might lose 125 lbs. from a bizarre, flesh-eating disease or get a gift certificate for liposuction. Disco music could come back. If it does, I'll be set.

There are new forms of hoarding emerging as we speak. The information age has spawned E-hoarding. E-hoarding is collecting thousands of unused software programs, emails, photo attachments, videos, MP3s, iPhone apps and links to web pages that no longer exist. Even though I've upgraded my computer ten times, I still have every email I've ever sent since the day I bought my first one in 1986 and the original user's manuals for DOS 1.0, WordPerfect 1.0 and VisiCalc.

I don't think I have a hoarding problem (although it's obvious I'm hording stories about hoarders). Compared to others on A&E's *Hoarders* and The Learning Channel's *Buried Alive*, I appear to be relatively normal. But, if I did have a crisis, it's comforting to know that there are experts who could help me with my problem: doctors, psychiatrists, psychologists, Hoarders Anonymous, closet organizers, certified professional organizers and Feng Sui consultants. People who can help pry those Richard Simmons VHS tapes from my cold, dead hands.

With Rentals Like These, Who Needs Friends?

This started out as a bad year. In less than six months, I lost my job, condominium, car and girlfriend. Even the cat packed up her litter box and left. When my parents heard the bad news, they immediately snapped into action: they fled to Boca Raton and dropped me from their Christmas card list. The exodus continued with all of my aunts, uncles, nieces and nephews and my one remaining frat brother. Then it hit me. Friends and relatives are just things. Things you can rent.

After the devastation settled in, I made up my mind that I was never going to own friends or family again. If I couldn't rent someone, I didn't need them. The following Monday, I began rebuilding my life.

I knew the first thing I'd need was a girlfriend. Someone to share the essence of life –holding hands and laughing while we skipped along the beach, picking up my dirty laundry, doing the vacuuming, cooking, and cleaning the bathroom in my pathetic little studio apartment. Maybe even someone to argue with when the urge moves me. So, I went directly to Rent-a-Friend.com.

There are a number of companies that rent girlfriends to life-long bachelors, philandering husbands or anyone else who wants all the benefits of saying "I do" with none of the commitments of uttering "I will." I looked into Rent-a-Friend.com because they were an international firm with a reputation for providing wholesome family values to men and women from all walks of life. I was also attracted to Rent-a-Friend because you can choose a woman who shares your interests. From rock climbing to going to football games, getting sloshed at night clubs, engaging in phone sex—all the things my last girlfriend never wanted to do. They'll even lie to your parole officer if you ask them.

Another advantage of renting a girlfriend from Rent-a-Friend was having offices in 42 countries around the world. Why should I pay for two airline tickets, extra baggage and everything else that goes along with vacationing with your girlfriend, when I can have a stand-in waiting for me at my destination? I'll save a bundle.

In addition to my rented girlfriend, I occasionally find myself in the position of needing a gorgeous woman to accompany me to upscale events like the Academy Awards. What to do? That's where Al Lampkin Entertainment comes in. Al Lampkin Entertainment is in the business of renting celebrities to nobodies like me for the evening. For a mere $1,000,000, I can be seen hanging out with Annie Lennox, Carrie Underwood, Chaka Khan, Britney Spears or Hillary Duff. And when I really want to get people talking around the water cooler, I opt for the additional obnoxious entourage of paparazzi, complete with blinding flashes and teenage girls jumping up down, screaming for my autograph.

Once I settled in with my rental girlfriend, I thought it would be fun to have an open house so that my friends could see my new digs. The only problem was I didn't have any. Fortunately, not having any friends or relatives isn't a problem these days—just rent them.

I went back to Rent-a-Friend and spoke with Charmaine about my situation. "Rent-a-Friend has packages for everyone, ranging from the small nuclear family to the large brood with dozens of grandkids," said Charmaine. She suggested that since I was starting over with a cheap rented apartment, I begin with the Basic Family

Sampler. "The Basic Family Sampler consists of a slightly alcoholic father, a Jewish mother puffed up on Botox, a sister in therapy and two senile grandparents—all for only $499 a month." She was even nice enough to throw in a teen-age daughter who hated me, for free. "Additional brothers and sisters are available with 3 hour minimums. Mothers-in-law, chain-smoking aunts and obnoxious next-door neighbors can also be rented by the hour, day or week. And, everything you spend on rental fees goes towards purchasing them, should you wish to do so." I don't know why I'd want to do something like that.

Since it had been so long since I had anything that resembled a normal conversation within a cohesive family, Charmaine suggested that I start with the 900-Minute Plan. "The 900-Minute Plan let's you spend up to 900 minutes a month conversing with any members of your rented family," said Charmaine. "After 9:00 PM, you can talk to each other for free. Conversations on the weekend are unlimited and any minutes you don't use, roll over to the next month."

Three months after my new family settled in, my daughter Beatrice announced at the dinner table that she was 3 months pregnant and had to get married. "Great," I said. "Another monthly rental to feed." The first thing I did was to complain to Charmaine about renting me a defective daughter. "Technically, Beatrice's pregnancy isn't a defect," she said. "It happens to lots of 16 year old girls who ride with the Hells Angels." She insisted that I'd have to rent Beatrice, her baby and her old man as a set. She couldn't split them up.

It's been five years since I've started my new rented life. I'm ecstatic. With the money I'm saving by not having to pay condominium association dues, property taxes, car payments or supporting real friends and relatives, I can easily afford my rental fees. Add to that all the money I'm saving on birthday presents throughout the year and I'm coming out miles ahead. Thank you Rent-a-Friend!

Wonder Butts and Instant Face Lifts

Somewhere around age 40, I acknowledged a harsh fact of life: gravity is wreaking havoc with my body—everything that was once up there is now down here. No amount of dieting, exercise or pills will reverse the trend. The only solution appears to be a radical one—cosmetic surgery. And, it's usually expensive. A simple butt lift could run thousands of dollars, is painful and there's no guarantee that it will last. That's why I was so excited when I bought the **Wonder Butt Bra** I saw advertised in the back of the Saturday Evening Post

The Wonder Butt Bra is a simple, unisex, one-size-fits-all device that's designed to lift and support my saggy keister. The same one that has suffered endless hours spread across my office cubicle, living room Lazy Boy and forced to endure never-ending, cross-country Meccas to my mother-in-law's house. Acting like a rock climber's sling, the Wonder Butt Bra's sturdy nylon belt circles my waist and is secured by a construction-grade belt buckle. Hanging below the waist belt are two loops that "catch" my sagging gluteals. I simply pull up on the adjustable belts until my buttocks sit as high as I want.

I immediately recognized the advantages of owning a Wonder Butt Bra. First, it's unisex, so I could borrow my wife's if I forgot mine at my girlfriend's. I could also start out slowly. One of the problems with having a facelift or other cosmetic surgery is the change is always so radical—one day you look like Mick Jagger and the next day you make Sheryl Crow look like Angelina Jolie. With the Wonder Butt Bra, I can start by cinching up my gluteals a little at a time. So slowly, that people may actually mistake me for someone who's started to work out.

Of course there are some downsides to the Wonder Butt Bra. If I forget to pack it before leaving on a long business trip, I'm out of luck. It's not like major department stores carry them. Oh sure, I can always pinch-hit with a roll of duct tape, but it never feels the same and the adhesive catches on my pubic hair. I'm also restricted to wearing the Wonder Butt Bra with certain types of clothing. Thongs and low-cut bathing suits are out. So is sunbathing in the nude. Even though the manufacturer is promising Wonder Butt Bras in new "flesh colored" models, I'm still limited to wearing beachwear like pedal pushers and clam diggers. I also can't undress in front of my doctor or strangers at the gym.

There's also a pretty good chance that I'll wear out my Wonder Butt Bra after subjecting it to unrelenting levels of high tensile stress so I'll need to think about buying a replacement even though I just bought my first one.

Even with its drawbacks, at $29.99, the Wonder Butt Bra has turned out to be a wonderful investment in my self-esteem. After all, I'm not likely to begin a life-changing fitness program any time soon, and no matter what I do, gravity continues to take its downward toll. Let's just hope the folks at Wonder Butt Bra continue to stay around for a while.

Another product that caught my eye promised to make me look younger overnight. With face lifts involving thousands of dollars and weeks of painful recovery, it's nice that someone has finally come up with an interim solution: the **Instant Face Lift**.

The Instant Face Lift was attractive to me because it truly was instant. I began by sliding the patented Anchor Band through my hair from front to back and gluing it in place using the specially designed surgical adhesive. The manufacturer warns against using nails, staples, Crazy Glue or commercial adhesives other than what comes with the Instant Face Lift kit. The other limitation I noticed was you have to have medium to long hair to cover the Anchor Band. But, that's a small price to pay for taking years off my appearance. If worse comes to worse, I could cash in my 401(k) and go for those hair plugs I've had my eye on.

Once I secured the Anchor Band in place, I glued the 6 tension tabs in place on the side of my face, using the special surgical cement. I glued the first tab just behind my eyebrow, one just in front of my ear and another to the angle of my jaw, just below the tip of my ear. After the glue dried, I pulled the other end of the tension straps up toward the Anchor Band and Velcroed the entire unit in place. Voila! Applied correctly, none of the glued tabs should be visible to others—especially when I wear a ski hat or football helmet. And for that occasional oriental look, I can apply a little extra tension to the strap behind my eyes. I can mix it up. Have a little fun!

There are, of course, a couple of drawbacks to using the Instant Face Lift. First, I'll need to keep my hair long, so I won't be joining the Navy SEALS, after all. Second, I can't wear the Instant Face Lift while getting my hair cut or having major brain surgery. Other than that, the Instant Face Lift looks great and has been an affordable way to take years off my appearance.

I work in a crowded office and frequently find myself working shoulder to shoulder in confined spaces. When I have to let loose the occasional air biscuit or Arkansas barking spider it can be a real problem. Oh sure, there are a number of great anti-gas products like Bean-O, Gas-X Extra Strength, Maalox Anti-gas chewable tablets, Phazyme, Flatulex and Simethicone, but I still need to remember to take them. And what happens if they don't do the job? Fortunately, there is a better solution—**The Gas Grabber**.

The Gas Grabber is a handy charcoal filtering pad that I slip inside the crotch of my underwear—on those rare occasions that I wear any. One side of the Gas Grabber has a peel-off backing so it will stay in place all day—even through vegetarian wedding receptions, running from the police and other physical activities where it's easy to float a trouser cough. At the end of the day, I just peel the Gas Grabber off of my underwear and throw it into the wash along with my other unmentionables.

Each Gas Grabber is loaded with high-capacity, charcoal deodorizing crystals designed to handle 12 or more bottom burps and comes in small, medium and large sizes. There's even a low profile model I can wear underneath hip huggers or on bare skin. For butt trumpeters whose farts are accompanied with loud, audible sounds, I'd recommend the new Anal Acoustic model. Tested in wind tunnels by audiologists, the Anal Acoustic Gas Grabber can mute offensive muff puffs up to 70 decibels—about the same noise level as an electric hair dryer.

One of my favorite ways to relax is to load up my sport utility vehicle with fishing poles, reels and tackle boxes filled with thousands of dollars of lures, lead weights, stinky bait, squirming worms, extra rolls of line and nets, storage creels and ice chests for a little bit of fishing. The problem is I never seem to catch anything.

After spending hours sitting in a boat or on the side of the river under the blistering sun, swatting away mosquitoes, I rarely catch a fish large enough to feed one member of my family. It's frustrating. I just wish there was an easier way. Fortunately, there is—**The Electro Fisher**.

The Electro Fisher is an ingenious piece of sports equipment that is guaranteed to bring in the fish. With my busy schedule, I've never really learned how to fish properly. So, I don't know the difference between a fly rod and a fly swatter. But it doesn't matter with The Electro Fisher. I can be an experienced angler in a matter of minutes.

The secret to The Electro Fisher is its high voltage fishing "wand." I just attach the Fishing Wand to the patented battery pack and I'm ready to go. Each high voltage Fishing Wand throws out 1,000 volts of killer electricity over a twenty-foot diameter. Just dip the Fishing Wand into the water and throw the switch. Within minutes, I have dozens of Brook, Rainbow and Cutthroat trout bobbing on the surface of the water, ready to pick up with my bare hands. No more tedious knot tying, spending hundreds of dollars on expensive lures or exhausting myself by whipping my fishing pole back and forth.

In addition to being the most effective fishing tool on the water, The Electro Fisher also has convenient electrical outlets for my iPod, laptop computer and an optional mini-frig I can stock with beer—or fish, if there's room. For those after the total outdoor experience, The Electro Fisher also comes with rubberized hip boots to protect you from electrocuting yourself while standing in the water. What I really enjoy is there's nothing to clean or repair. The Electro Fisher folds up into a lightweight pouch, ready to slide underneath my bunk at the cheesy motel room I've rented for the week.

There's nothing I enjoy more than cruising down the Pacific Coast Highway on my motorcycle with the wind whipping through my hair. But, when I get back to the teeming city, the risk of having an accident comes from every angle. True, motorcycle helmets, leather chaps and jackets offer some protection in the event of an accident, but they're hot, difficult to move around in and can't fortify me against teenage girls rear-ending me while texting their BFF. Fortunately, there is a more effective alternative—the **Motorcycle Airbag**.

The Motorcycle Airbag is an ingenious invention that is designed to give motorcycle riders and their passengers full body protection. It works like the pressure suits of the early days of flight-testing. I simply slip into the Motorcycle Airbag and zip it up the front. After buckling the durable web belt, I clip the end of the bungee belt onto a secure location on the motorcycle—like the hot end of an exhaust pipe. In the event that I'm hit, the bungee cord snaps tight and sets off a series of compact air canisters that inflate the air bag. Even my head is protected, because the collar inflates into a full-head motorcycle helmet.

The Motorcycle Airbag has been wind tunnel tested by the AAA in crashes up to 300 mph and shown to be a superior alternative to other forms of motorcycle safety equipment and clothing. Granted, it won't save my life, but the Airbag will keep all of my body parts in tact so the Highway Patrol and Paramedics needn't look far to round up all of my dismembered arms and legs. When not in use, the Airbag can be deflated to look just like a kilo of cocaine and stored inside my leather jacket next to my handgun.

When you're in the mood for a ride, leave the helmet, chaps and hot leathers at home. Just grab your Motorcycle Airbag and head for the open highway!

Stranded in Purgatory

Here I am. Stranded in Purgatory. You'd think with all of the opportunities I've had to excel or fall from grace, I'd have gone straight to Heaven or Hell. Instead, I'm trapped here in mediocrity.

Getting stranded in Purgatory is the equivalent of getting a C+ on your Chemistry final—not bad, but not great, either. True, I've never gone out of my way for anyone, my entire life. Faced with the opportunity to do something illegal, compassionate or meaningful that could result in some form of positive or negative distinction, I've always taken the easy way out. Like the time Morrie Fensterman's wife came onto me at the Christmas party. Instead of ripping off her elf costume and ravishing her on the conference table, I chose to give her a half-assed hickey in the janitor's closet. Big deal. "You'll never get into heaven that way," accused my pastor. Apparently, it won't get me into hell, either. Where it *did* get me was the head of the line to Purgatory. You have to do something a lot worse than having a tussle with your manager's wife to earn a lifetime of eternal fire.

I knew all about Purgatory from the sixth grade. Every Sunday after mass, my mother stuffed me behind a desk in Sister Mary Blanchefleur's catechism class. As she patrolled the aisles, she scolded us for our sinful ways and threatened to send us to Purgatory. I didn't know what that meant, but it sounded worse than going straight to Heaven, but not as bad as going to Hell, so I knew I still had some wiggle room in the way I lived my life. I could probably continue taking swigs off of Uncle Bert's Jack Daniels bottle, but I should probably quit setting the cat's tail on fire. Besides, I was still young. I had plenty of time to mend my ways before I died of a heart attack, sitting at my desk at age 65. Or, so I thought.

As it turns out, my life on earth came to an end sooner than I anticipated. While rock climbing in Yosemite, I was showing off in front of Bethany Lieberman, when I misjudged the width of a granite ledge and plunged to my death in a matter of seconds. It's true what they say about seeing your life passing before you on the way down. It gives you time to review your entire existence—who you've screwed and who has screwed you—before you enter the hereafter. In some cases, you can even make amends to people before you hit ground, but that's more along the lines of swiping someone's parking space than bilking Bernie Madoff out of his life's savings.

The word Purgatory comes from the Latin term, *Purgatorium*, which means "to spend a thousand years with your mother-in-law" and is used to refer to any non-specific place of temporary suffering. Before I was allowed to enter Purgatory, I had to go through a fairly rigorous registration process, filling out one form after another with my name, religious affiliation, age, cause of death and a brief description of how I spent my time on Earth. They want to make sure that a) you're not Anglican, Protestant, Lutheran or Methodist and b) you weren't already slated for the expressway to Hell. Apparently, some guy named Hitler slipped through the cracks and managed to stay here for almost 3 months. It caused quite a ruckus. That was over 50 years ago and they're still talking about it.

After I was cleared for entry, the angels (who turned out to be exterminated TSA agents) divided us into two groups—the hopeless cases who were riddled with mortal sin and those who were merely tarnished with venial offenses. Even though stabbing your neighbor in the back has relative levels of severity on earth, they're not so lenient in Purgatory. Mortal sinners get their first inkling of their ultimate destination when they take away their winter clothes, give them a thong and a large tube of SPF 850,000 sunscreen. Those of us who had committed relatively minor infractions like slipping Ecstasy into my babysitter's Coke, were able to keep our clothes and were shackled to a ball and chain with an image of God emblazoned with, "I'm with him."

The first real surprise came to me when I heard screaming coming from the cleansing chambers. I was under the impression that I'd be getting a hot shower, shampoo and maybe a deep-tissue massage to wash away my sins prior to leaving for Heaven. Evidently I was a little more naughty than I thought because I was scheduled for a several rounds of deep cleansing starting the next morning. During deep cleansing, they chained me to one of the bloodstained walls near the torture chambers and burned off my sins using a flamethrower. The pain wasn't quite as bad as sitting through Sister Mary Blanchefleur's catechism classes, but close. Allowing time for your skin to grow back, the entire process usually takes several weeks—depending on what you did while you were on Earth. I knew the only way they were going to rid me of the experience of wearing my aunt's false teeth for Halloween was through multiple cleansing sessions—and a good round with the belt sander.

After a week of enduring lectures and repeated deep cleansing, I began to get impatient and asked a few of the angels when they thought I might be getting out and moving up to Heaven. "No one really knows," they said. "We found a prayer roll belonging to Henry VIII that claimed to reduce his time here by 52,712 years." Fifty-two thousand years! There was no way I'd be able to make it that long. Besides, Henry VIII had a LOT more baggage when he got here than I did. Beheading Ann Boleyn had to be worth a few thousand years, just by itself.

The next day I got some more bad news. Apparently, I'd have to go through a few more hoops before getting out of Purgatory. Including time already served, my remaining stay would be divided into 7 levels while ascending Mt. Purgatory. The seven levels weren't anything like working my way through ski school. Each was designed to help me conquer one of the 7 deadly sins. And, each time I entered a higher level, I had to pay a toll. Great. Not only was I going to have to confront lust and gluttony all over again, I'd have to scrounge around for spare change from some of the other residents.

"Don't be so despondent," said the angels. "You can get out of here faster if you have people back on earth praying for you." Fat chance. I never even prayed for my grandparents after they drove off that bridge and drowned, so it wasn't likely that someone like me was going to rack up many prayers from my so-called friends back on earth. Oh sure, when I was in the ICU recovering from a heroin overdose they promised me, "We'll pray for you," but they never do. Where were they now when I really needed them?

After a couple more weeks, the angels told me that I was making good progress and my stay shouldn't be much longer. I met a couple of guys named Saddam and Osama who said they'd be happy to help me get through wrath and greed before they left for Hell, but I'd have to find someone else for the rest of my sins.

As it turned out, I finally got a seat on the bus for Heaven leaving the following morning. I managed to qualify for an early release program because Purgatory was just bursting at the seams. They needed to make room for an incoming load of celebrities and personalities—some people named Manson, Simpson and an ice skater named Harding.

Reincarnation Gone Cluck

For the life of me, I can't figure out how I got here. A month ago, I was contentedly adjusting to my short stay in Purgatory, waiting for the bus to Heaven. Then, out of the blue—poof—I find myself standing in the middle of Mandelbaum's Commercial Poultry Farm in Bakersfield, California. Both are a long way from Heaven.

My life came to an abrupt end during a fluke rock climbing accident in Yosemite National Park. Given my vile and contemptible life on Earth, it came as no surprise that I'd be sent to Purgatory before I made it past the pearly gates. But, nobody told me about reincarnation. Granted, they said there was an outside chance I'd be forced to spend a little more time on earth before rising to the great beyond, but Mandelbaum's Poultry Farm? C'mon. Give me a break. Even Leona Helmsley got to enjoy 3 weeks as a Burmese belly dancer before they shipped her off to Hell.

I was dropped into the middle of a chicken coop on a busy Friday afternoon in the form of a mature Rhode Island Red—eight and half pounds of pure Chicken McNuggets. Most of the management had already gone home for the Labor Day weekend, so there weren't any humans around to complain to. Instead, I was left to my own devices to secure my spot in a pecking order of 8,000 other mature hens and roosters. Looking back, I suppose it could have been worse. If I had arrived a week earlier, I might have already been cut up and slathered with Bar-B-Que sauce on someone's holiday party platter. Or, I might have awakened to find my skewered carcass slowly circling the rotisserie grill in a Gelson's Market. At least this way, I'd have a couple of days to get to know some of the locals before formulating an escape plan.

The first one to approach me was a 3-year-old Wyandotte hen with a sexy, bright red wattle. "Allen? Is that you? It's me. Hannah Rifkin. From high school!" Although it was hard to distinguish her features underneath the layers of feathers, I recognized that whiny voice from the five hours we spent together at my senior prom. "Hannah, how are you? You look wonderful. Life has been good to you." "Aw, you're just being nice, Allen. Ever since laying those 400 eggs, I just haven't been able to get this extra weight off." Hannah spent the remainder of the afternoon showing me around the chicken coop until the sun went down and it was time for the Shabbat meal.

"I've got to get out of here," I told Hannah the next morning. "This has all been a terrible mistake. I didn't even finish my deep cleaning sessions in Purgatory. And I still have to finish my workbook lessons on wrath and greed before they'll let me into Heaven. What happens if they ship me off to some mid-west KFC? My life will be over!"

"Well, Allen," said Hannah. "I hate to be the one to tell you this, but your life as you knew it is already over. The best thing you can do is relax, have some more chicken feed and I'll introduce you to a few of the other roosters around the pool. On Monday, the staff will be back, they'll sex you and decide where you belong."

I was absolutely beside myself. I was miles away from home, lost my wallet, iPhone and Kindle and was badly in need of a Xanax. I hadn't spoken to either my publisher or therapist in over 10 days and was 3 weeks behind writing my memoirs. To make matters worse, there wasn't a laptop or WiFi hotspot within 50 miles. I had no way of sending anyone an email to let them know what was going on. And, without fingers, I'd be reduced to hunting and pecking on a keyboard—literally. That's assuming I could find a Starbucks with rental terminals.

Monday morning, the staff showed up hung over from the long holiday weekend. It wasn't likely they were going to be sympathetic to the story of a full-grown rooster dropping out of the sky from Purgatory into Mandelbaum Farms, but I had to give it a try. I had to make a break for it.

"So, you don't think you belong at Mandelbaum Farms, do you?" said Feibush. Feibush Gavel was the General Manager at Mandelbaum Farms. "No, there's been a terrible mistake," I said. "I'm supposed to be on my way to Heaven." "Well, I've heard that before," said Feibush. "You know, you could do worse. Some of the souls that dropped down from Purgatory never got a chance to be a Church's chicken dinner or even an order of TGIF Chicken Fingers. They were sold for Hindu cremation ceremonies or cockfights. Some of the others ended up being sacrificed during Santerian rituals or slaughtered for a kapparos."

I gasped. "But I have a master's degree in Hebrew and Aramaic Cultures. And, I haven't paid off my student loans. My credit scores have probably gone down the tubes by now. There must be something you can do for me."

Feibush thought about my predicament. He hated sending a college-educated capon out to become an order of hot wings. Instead, he made me Manager in Charge of the free-range herds. It was my job to interview new chicks and determine if they were qualified to roam freely on the ranch. This involved running background checks and pre-employment drug screenings. The hardest part of the job was getting a 12-week-old chick to pee in a plastic cup.

After 7 years, my sight began to go, so Feibush shipped me off to the Mandelbaum Farms Retirement Home for Aging Poultry, where I lived out the rest of my life. Eventually, I was invited up to Heaven, where I while away the day, swapping stories with some of my friends who didn't fare as well as I. I love hearing their stories of escaping deep fryers and boiling peanut oil-filled woks. I consider myself fortunate to be a college-educated pecker. Things could have been a lot worse.

Smoke 'em if Ya Got 'em

When I was sixteen, my biggest goal in life was to learn how to smoke. Not because I thought it was particularly good for me, but because hanging around a street corner, sucking on a cigarette butt commanded all the respect any post-pubescent male could possibly expect out of life. And, who *wouldn't* respect someone for spending their allowance on something that was not only disgusting but turned their teeth yellow, gave them bad breath, made their clothes reek and was almost guaranteed to kill them?

Lighting up my first cigarette was everything I thought it would be and more—like circling my lips around the exhaust pipe of an 18-wheeler as the driver stepped on the gas. The hot fumes singed the lining of my throat and fried my palate as they scorched their way to my lungs. I loved it.

When I enlisted in the Navy, I found that smoking cigarettes was essential to survival. Several times a day, the drill instructor would yell out, "Smoke break. Smoke 'em if ya got 'em." If you didn't got 'em, he'd soon find some distasteful task for you to do like scrubbing the inside of garbage cans, so eventually we all took up smoking.

In all fairness, I didn't get hooked on cigarettes all by myself. I had the Marlboro Man to thank for that. Throughout history, when soldiers returned home from military conflicts, Madison Avenue made sure that they were right there with them. After years of living in swamps and trenches, they wanted to show G.I.s how much fun they could have prancing around a tennis court or golf course with a lit cigarette in their mouth. Lucky Strike was the first out of the gate in the 1940s with ads featuring men and women at their country club, enjoying their new found freedom: "What a day! What a game! What a cigarette! Why is Lucky so much a part of moments like this?"

Tobacco companies soon learned that enlisting big name stars like John Wayne and Ronald Reagan was an effective way to glorify cigarette smoking. During the promotion of his 1954 film, "Big Jim McClain," The Duke sat comfortably on the set with a cigarette dangling from his fingers: "Mild and good tasting, pack after pack. And I should know. I've been smokin' em for twenty years."

Another up and coming actor with political aspirations promised, "Want to be the next President? Just do what Ronald Reagan does—smoke lots and lots of Pall Mall brand cigarettes! The sooner you start, the faster you'll rise to political success!"

It wasn't until 1977 that I finally decided to ignore the advice of John Wayne and Ronald Reagan and do something good for my health—I tried to quit smoking. After I got swept up in the jogging craze, I found that it was almost impossible to run while simultaneously hacking up a lung. You rarely saw a skinny Ethiopian crossing the finish line of the Boston Marathon with a Camel dangling from his lips. Cigarette smoking and jogging made incompatible bedfellows, so one of them would have to go. The question was which one?

In those days, there weren't any shortcuts to quitting—no Chantix, Topamax, Zyban, Nicoderm, Nicorette, Nicotrol, Habitrol, Buproban, Aventyl, Nicotrol, Commit or Nicorelief—just hard core will power. For a while, I found it helpful to suck on my thumb, but when I started losing all of my friends I decided to switch to pacifiers, twigs and even pencils. They were sort of like having a cigarette in your mouth, but almost impossible to keep lit. The rest of the time I just walked around in nicotine withdrawal, hyperventilating into brown paper bags and hoping the anxiety and despair would pass before I took my own life.

Then, it dawned on me that there was no reason why I should have to give up a habit I loved so much, all at once. After all, if you're overweight, your doctor doesn't tell you to quit eating. No. He tells you to start cutting back on your calories. So, instead of quitting smoking cold turkey, I decided to try tapering off. How hard could it be? Except for the first cigarette in the morning, the two or three at mid-morning, the two after lunch, the three in the afternoon, the six with cocktails, the one after dinner and the two or three while watching television and getting ready for bed, I could do without smoking.

Over a series of months, I gradually dispensed with smoking a whole cigarette in one sitting. Instead, I'd take a few puffs, then pinch off the burning embers, tucking it behind my ear for later. I began squirreling away partially smoked butts in secret hiding places and making up excuses to leave the dinner table for a quick toke. I had butts hidden everywhere—in the glove compartment of the car, inside my ski boots and in my French horn case in the attic. My girlfriend began to suspect that I was seeing someone else behind her back. She couldn't understand why I had to play the French horn every time we had sex. When I finally ran out of plausible explanations, she left me for someone else. Probably a non-smoker.

All it took was a few puffs of glorious nicotine to see me through. But, as long as I bought cigarettes a pack at a time, the threat of completely relapsing was my constant companion. Ultimately, I found a seedy liquor store at the beach that would sell me one cigarette at a time for a dollar. The 1-cigarette-a-day habit digressed to ¾ to ½ to eventually ¼, spread carefully over the course of an entire day. I kept that up for nearly 6 months.

I finally did quit smoking. I think what really did it for me was reflecting on all the time I was wasting hanging out with Chester, Mad Dog and the hookers down at the Ocean Front Liquor Store.

Over time, I became one of those born again, ex-smoking runners. I learned to despise that phlegmy hack that only a 3-pack a day smoker can produce when laughing at a good joke. Without my ties to cigarette smoking, I even started buying tank tops and T-shirts without pockets. I must have matured a bit, as well. I didn't give one thought to whether or not I looked cool. Being alive trumps looking cool any day of the week.

Happy Birthday to Me

I just celebrated another birthday. Now, before you start applauding, you need to understand that at my age, birthdays aren't something I relish with any level of enthusiasm. To me, birthdays merely mark the passage of time. The only thing I do to achieve another year on Earth is continue breathing in and out and swing my feet out of bed each morning—which is becoming more difficult than it sounds.

Things were simpler before the rise of Christianity. People didn't know how to calculate the lunar calendar, so they couldn't keep track of birthdays. Everyone just assumed they were getting older when they couldn't see their toes any more. Then, Facebook took over the Internet, forcing you to remember when your friends were born. Nevertheless, by the end of my special day this year, I hadn't heard from a single relative or high school chum. I did, however, get a tweet from my periodontist, an automated call from a roofing company and a festive postcard from my proctologist reminding me it was time for my 5-year colonoscopy. Sort of makes you feel all warm and fuzzy inside.

In the beginning, birthday celebrations were reserved for kings, pharaohs and other high-ranking officials who could afford superfluous celebrations during a weak economy. People weren't expected to bring gifts when invited to birthday parties. Their mere presence was counted on as they surrounded the guest of honor to ward away evil spirits. To insure that the spirits stayed away, two teacher-sisters, Patty and Mildred Hill, penned the tune "Good Morning to All" in 1893, which was abruptly renamed to "Happy Birthday to You" and sung to all their students. Rumor has it that the mere sound of the elderly teachers' voices kept all of their students safe—at least until they graduated or got married the first time. What many people don't know is that the song was copy written and purchased by Warner Chappell in 1935. To this day, it's technically illegal to sing "Happy Birthday" in public without paying royalties to his estate, which is why you seldom hear it sung in restaurants and other businesses anymore. That and the fact that American college students can't remember the words.

Some attribute the first birthday cake to the Greeks. They would bake treats to offer up to the moon goddess Artemis. Early Germans commemorated children's birthdays during "Kinderfest," by letting the child of honor lay around the house the entire day, skipping their chores and homework. The custom has become so popular that it's spread like wildfire around the world and is now considered a permanent part of American culture.

The British still have a quaint custom of putting thimbles and coins in the batter of the cake before being baked. They believe that the guest who bites down into the piece of cake containing a coin will inherit great wealth. The guest who bites down into a piece of cake with the thimble will never marry. And, the guest who bites down into the piece of cake, shattering their crown, will get a new root canal.

A number of countries enjoy festive customs that put Americans to shame. In Ghana, children are treated on their birthday to an "oto"—a yummy surprise made from mashed sweet potatoes and eggs. Mmmm mmm. Kenyan children look forward the entire year to celebrating their birthdays in dirty, rat-infested barns alongside the family's cattle. The Nepalese have their foreheads smeared with a colorful blend of rice and yogurt and Irish children languish in the custom of "bumping," where the adults hoist the guest of honor upside down by their ankles and bump their heads on the floor—an equal number of drops for each year on Earth. My parents adopted the custom when I was five and still practice it every year at my birthday party—usually when they're looking for change for cigarettes.

Taking the lead from their Irish neighbors, Canadian birthday honorees receive an equal number of punches as their years on earth. While I suppose it's easy enough for youngsters to suck up a dozen or so punches, there's something pathetic about the practice of pummeling your grandmother 83 times on her arm to celebrate her birth.

The most perplexing custom comes from the Latin American countries where parents save their entire lives, working three jobs around the clock, hocking everything they have of value and taking out a second mortgage on their home to pay for a "Quinceañera," on their daughter's 15th birthday. Then, ten years later, they're expected to cough up another $50,000 for her wedding.

So, Veels geluk met jou verjaarsdag, Taredartzet shnorhavor, Ois guade winsch i dia zum Gbuadsdog or Happy Birthday to you! If you were born on this day, get ready to be smacked, pulled and dowsed with strange liquids while you're eating things even barnyard animals wouldn't touch. It's your day!

Monkey in a Pink Canoe

"Where did I come from?" asked Shadrach as we pulled up to his football game at Fleigenbaum Field. Having never been married, I thought I'd be exempt from ever having this discussion with a 6-year-old quarterback, so I never put much thought into what I'd say if asked. Looks like I was going to have to punt.

"Well, Shadrach, each month, in one of your mommy's two ovaries, a few immature eggs develop into follicles. The mature follicle releases an egg during ovulation, which turns into the corpus luteum. Progesterone prepares the endometrium in anticipation of the embryo. Then, your daddy's sperm travels up the fallopian tube where it fertilizes your mommy's egg, mixing her X chromosomes with his Y chromosomes to create a zygote and blastocyst. Thanks to Human Chorionic Gonadotrophin, nine months later you were born!"

"I just meant what *town* was I born in?" said Shadrach. "Meshach said it was Toledo, but Abednego thinks it was Cleveland."

Since I'd already opened the door to the wonders of human reproduction, Shadrach had me cornered for "the discussion."

Evidently, neither of his parents wanted to get involved. I don't blame them. My father never sat me down, either. Instead, he just sent me into my bedroom with a stack of National Geographics and told me to figure it out myself. I learned the rest from Tommy Flugelman while walking to school.

I decided to take the conservative approach by mixing simple human reproductive biology with basic street knowledge. "Based on whether we're a boy or a girl, each of us is born with some basic equipment. Boys have a monkey and girls have a beaver. When your mommy wants something special from your daddy (like $4,500 for that fur coat she saw at Macy's), she'll let daddy's monkey play with her beaver." I could tell that this made no sense to Shadrach, so I asked him to be patient and hang in with me. It would all come together soon.

"Is that when I hear all the screaming coming from mommy and daddy's bedroom?" asked Shadrach. "It sounds like he's hurting her."

"Yes. That's right," I said. "But, mommy actually likes it when your daddy lets his monkey out. In fact, mommy likes it so much, when daddy is at work and she's home all alone, she *imagines* that daddy's monkey is playing with her beaver. She calls it tickling the taco, paddling the pink canoe or parting the red sea."

"Will I ever learn how to tickle my taco?" he said. "I'm glad you asked that question, Shadrach. You see, boys are different from girls. While you don't have a beaver or a taco, you do have a bald-headed yogurt slinger. Sometimes we refer to it as a bologna pony, one-eyed trouser snake, pocket rocket or Russell the love muscle. With those, you get to choke the chicken, flick your bean, slap the salami, polish your knob, spank your monkey or shake the creamer. But, you have to be careful, Shadrach. If you flog your log too much, you'll grow hair on the palms of your hands and everyone will know what you do when you're alone in your bedroom."

"This morning," he said "my one-eyed trouser snake was pointing straight out of my pajamas and left a pool of man chowder on the sheets—or at least that's what Tommy calls it. Has that ever happened to you?" I told him, "There's nothing wrong with waking up in the morning to a little baby gravy in your jammies. They call it a wet dream and it just means that your man plumbing works. But, I wouldn't leave your bedroom until it crawls back into your peejays."

Shadrach thought that over for a minute, then came up with another one.

"When Uncle Phil slept over during Passover, I noticed that his body was *covered* with hair. It was disgusting! Will that ever happen to me?" I thought about the question for a minute and told Shadrach he'd just have to wait until he got a little older to see. "Generally, if you start going bald by the time you're 25 or 30, the hair on top of your head will slide down to your back, shoulders and around your bologna pony. Some people think it's sexy."

"I know what you mean," said Shadrach. "I caught Uncle Phil's man friend kissing him all over and touching his pocket rocket. Then he tried to put his Russell muscle into Uncle Phil's brown-eyed Willy, but Uncle Phil said he couldn't because he didn't have a condom. I don't know what a condom is, but they ended up getting into a big fight and Uncle Phil's friend stomped out of the bedroom saying 'There will be no more Lewinskys for you.' I asked mommy what condoms and Lewinskys were while her Bridge Club was here. Mrs. Bickler turned bright red, fell off her chair and they had to call an ambulance to take her to the hospital. Then, mom locked me in my room. I never did find out what they were.

Sensing the discussion was taking an uncontrollable and hopefully unneeded trajectory, I tried to reel it back in by talking about the opposite sex.

"Shadrach, have you started to notice the girls at school yet?" He said he had, but he wasn't sure he liked what he saw. "Last year, Marisa Berkowitz used to be shorter than me, so I usually won all our wrestling matches behind the cafeteria. Over the summer, she got HUGE and grew a moustache. To make matters worse, she has these big bumps on her chest. She won't let me touch 'em, either. Will I grow bumps on my chest?"

I assured him that it was part of the natural growth process for girls Marisa's age and he shouldn't have to worry about that for a while. "When you get to be 65 or 70, you'll probably grow man tits, and have to wear a brassiere. But, wearing a bra at 70 years old will be the least of your worries. By that time you probably won't be able to pee anymore and your love stick will stop standing up on its own. If you want to continue playing hide the hot dog with your wife, you'll have to drop $400 a month on these little blue pills called Viagra just to make sure you'll be able to tickle her taco."

"Sheesh," said Shadrach. "Life gets really complicated when you get older, doesn't it?" I had to agree. Things are simpler when you're a child from somewhere in Ohio.

The Games People Play

Even if you don't like sports, it was hard not to get excited about the Summer Olympic Games held last year in London, England. The pageantry, the colorful uniforms and swapping pins with spectators from all over the world made it a must-see event. But, they didn't start out that way.

The Summer Olympic Games began as a handful of rag-tag wrestling matches held in a vacant dirt parking lot in 776 B.C. behind Nicodemus' Deli about the time Homer was born—that's Homer the Greek poet responsible for penning the Iliad and the Odyssey, not the cartoon patriarch of the Simpsons. Legend has it that the games were created to honor the God Zeus and to help men prepare for military battle—but that's where the similarity to the modern Olympic Games ends. You wouldn't have found flashy Chinese uniforms with snappy berets or Michael Johnson's solid gold sprinter's shoes on the feet of Herodoros of Megara or Aelius Granianus of Sikyon. In fact, the all-male athletes pranced around the stadium stark naked nude—which was probably why women were prohibited from competition. Since there were no "R" television ratings (or even televisions for that matter) and the porn industry was still thousands of years away, women were prohibited from watching the games in person or on premium channels through Direct TV.

Over the years, the original competitions have expanded from six simple feats of strength to more than 26 individual events contested on the ground, in the air, underwater, on grass, inside and outside of elaborate, multi-million-dollar athletic stadiums that ultimately wind up taking their place in history as second class bluegrass music venues and swap meets.

Boxing was one of the first competitions in the early Olympics. There were literally no weight classes between men and young boys and little else in the way of rules. When a boxer knocked his opponent to the ground, he was free to keep hitting and kicking him until they carried him away on a stretcher—the hittee, not the hitter. Pankration was a grueling combination of boxing and wrestling and probably planted the seeds for World Wrestling Entertainment. The rules were simple but slightly more refined than WWE bouts: opponents weren't allowed to bite or gouge each other's eyes out with their fingernails. But, you did have permission to break each other's fingers and throw sand in their eyes.

Then, of course, there were the Chariot Races, the Pentathlon and various running events, culminating in the 768-meter run where the athletes were required to sprint in full armor, including helmets, shields, shin guards and swords—but still no underwear.

Fast forward to the modern Olympic Games, we usually have to endure the host country's latest cockamamie demonstration events in hopes that they might someday find their way into the permanent lineup—like Table Tennis, Rhythmic Dancing and Synchronized Swimming. In fact, quite a few have tried. More than a few have failed.

The Paris Summer Olympic Games of 1900 provided a watershed of athletic hopefuls. The first one was Lawn Bowling. Heavy, metal balls (weighted on one side—God only knows why) were rolled down a grass-covered lawn to see who could get closest to the "Jack" or the "Kitty." Even though it's still watched on BBC by over three million enthusiasts, the International Olympic Committee felt that even watching paint dry on a wall was more exciting than Lawn Bowling, so they dropped it from contention.

In the same year, Hot Air Ballooning made its debut, but was ultimately eliminated because the spectators could never figure out the best venue to watch the competition. Long before helicopters, television, sky-cams and Jumbo Trons, thousands of fans would huddle around the starting line cheering on dozens of colorful balloons as they flew off into the sunset, never to be seen again. That was it. Back to the hotel.

The original Greek Tug of War was resurrected from the games of 500 B.C. According to the rules, eight men on each side strained and grunted, attempting to pull the opposing team six feet across the centerline. Because all of the contestants were so equally trained (this was long before anything like blood doping, human growth hormone and anabolic steroids gave one side a winning edge), the competition usually resulted in watching 16 men grunt, fart and spit in a Mexican standoff until the spectators got bored and left. As anticipated, the event was cancelled due to lack of interest.

Finally, there were two other competitions vying for the public's attention: Live Pigeon Shooting and the Plunge for Distance. Prior to the days of clay skeet shooting, a dozen competitors with shotguns stood at the ready, waiting for the officials to release more than 300 live pigeons into the air. The object was to shoot down as many birds as possible in the least amount of time. While a crack shot could surgically remove more than 20 birds, the majority of the contestants ended up decimating the flock, blanketing the countryside with a stomach-churning layer of mangled bird meat, blood and feathers.

But, by far, the most boring event was the Plunge for Distance. Competitors stood perched on top of a high diving platform over a deep swimming pool. When the signal was given, the contestant dove off the platform to the bottom of the pool where they lie motionless until they ran out of breath—which felt like years to the spectators watching from the sidelines. Eventually, the crowds grew bored watching a group of men lay on the bottom of a pool and left, leaving the divers clinging to life—their eyes fixed on the gold medal.

Since then, there have been dozens of other demonstration events that never made the grade: the 200m Obstacle Swimming Race, One Hand Weight Lifting, Glima Wrestling and Korfball. Many other sports such as Buzkaski, Shin Kicking, Wife Carrying and Ferret Legging are popular and played over the world—just not enough to find a permanent spot in the Summer Olympic Games. Maybe someday…

The Triple Nipple Club

I have three nipples. I'm not proud of them, but there they are. Resting a few inches below my right breast, my third nipple (also called a supernumerary nipple, accessory breast, multiple breast syndrome, mammae erraticae or polythelia) was first pointed out to me in the sixth grade when I took my shirt off during a heated kickball match. At the time, it was about the same size as my female classmates' nipples, so I was a little self-conscious about it. Since then, I've just accepted it and been glad it hasn't grown any larger.

As it turns out, having three nipples is more common than I originally thought. One in 18 men and 50 women has at least one extra nipple. Some famous people, including Mark Wahlberg, Lily Allen, Carrie Underwood and Tilda Swinton have them. Extra breasts (with or without lactating nipples) have had minor roles in the movies *The Warrior and the Sorceress*, *Total Recall*, *Star Trek V*, *Earth Girls are Easy*, *Firecracker*, *Flesh Gordon 2*, *Dumb and Dumber* and *Return of the Jedi*. They can show up anywhere on the body and during Tudor times were considered a mark of witchcraft. Urban legend has it that one woman had a third lactating nipple on the bottom of her foot. Fortunately for her, it's never been considered necessary to wear a bra over a third nipple—just the first two.

As a middle-age man, it's not likely that I'll be needing a third nipple anytime soon but having it surgically removed has been cost prohibitive, so when I go to the beach I just cover it up with a band-aid. I cover the other two with a T-shirt, pasties or my Wonder Bra.

During my polythelia research I ran across a number of other human anomalies that have plagued mankind over the past several hundred years. In 2006, a 24-year-old man checked himself into a New Delhi hospital to have his extra penis removed. Called *diphallia*, he wanted to have it expunged so he could marry his childhood sweetheart and have a normal sex life. Naturally, when I discovered that over 100 men have had multiple genitalia, it revved up my imagination. Just think of the benefits. If I was one of those fortunate souls with extra equipment, I could masturbate with both hands at the same time or switch off between the left and the right. I could reduce the wear and tear on my organs by alternating them on some type of schedule. Sort of like having your tires rotated at Walmart. Having two peckers would undoubtedly increase my chances of getting laid—even if just for the sake of curiosity. A lot of men can claim that they're "hung like a horse," but there aren't too many who can brag, "I've got two weenies."

In 1889, a resourceful man made a life-long career out of his attributes. Sicilian Francesco Lentini was born with three legs, two sets of genitals and an extra foot growing out of the knee of his third leg. As expected, he was the center of attention at his wedding reception. With three legs and feet, he single-handedly commandeered the dance floor. And his sexual performance on his wedding night has become the substance of legends. Turning his back on a prodigious soccer career, he used his special qualities to become famous by touring with the Ringling Brothers, Barnum & Bailey Circus and after marrying, raised a family of four children until he passed away in Florida at the ripe old age of 78. There's been no word whether or not his children inherited his special gifts. Even having just an extra finger would be a nice way to remember dad.

Hazel Jones, an attractive 27-year-old British woman has her own special qualities. After suffering from excruciating menstrual cramps, the then 18-year-old from High Wycombe discovered she had a condition called *didelphys*, or two vaginas. "It's not that crazy at all, even though it sounds like a sci-fi thing," said Vincenzo Berghella, Director of Maternal Fetal Medicine at Thomas Jefferson University in Philadelphia. "We see many women with two vaginas (which includes two separate uteruses and cervixes)—maybe one a month or more." According to the World Health Organization, one in every 3,000 women is born with the condition, although I've never been fortunate enough to date a single one. Jones never thought much of her duplicity until she experienced painful sex with her boyfriend. She was also puzzled by her friends' responses when she asked them, "Which hole do I put my tampon in?" She was referring to her two vaginas. They thought she was confused about the difference between her vagina and her rectum.

Even though it's easy to surgically correct the condition, many don't. "I thought it was amazing and it's definitely an ice-breaker at parties," said Jones. "If women want to have a look, I'm quite happy to show them," although I'm sure she wouldn't feel comfortable giving me a peek. Another young lady discovered there was an added benefit to having two vaginas—she lost her virginity twice—once on her wedding night and the other in the backseat of her Volvo.

If doctors would have discovered The Great Lentini's double penises the same time they stumbled upon Hazel Jones' dual vaginas, they might have been responsible for the longest marriage on record. With their unique equipment, it's unlikely that either of them would have gone outside their bedroom to explore better options.

After learning about double penises, dual vaginas and triple legs, I didn't feel nearly as self-conscious about my triple nipples as I once did, even if Mark Wahlberg, Carrie Underwood or Tilda Swinton do about theirs.

Shake My Hand or I'll Kiss You

Moments after I was born, Dr. Felsenbaum greeted me with a slap on my heinie. Naturally, I was too young to understand the significance of the gesture and took immediate offense to being manhandled straight out of the womb. As it turns out, it wouldn't be the last time someone slapped me on my backside.

That whack on the bum was my first introduction to a long list of quaint American greeting traditions and was meant to get me started crying and breathing. Of course, I didn't know that at the time. I would have preferred a hearty handshake followed by a request to exhale. If he'd asked, I would have been happy to comply—especially if he offered me a cigarette. But, like it or not, that's how my life began.

When I was in junior high school, we greeted all our friends with a unique variety of insults designed to generate attention—starting by pulling their underwear up to their shoulder blades. I remember being smacked on the back of my head so hard my retainer shot across the room. Slapping our girlfriends on the heinie was preferred over a hearty handshake and was considered a sign of affection. Everyone got away with it, but there's no way I'd consider giving my supervisor a flat or a wedgie, today.

Not being much of a world traveler, I was surprised to learn from the Discovery Channel that greeting strangers with a simple handshake isn't the only way people say hello. And it isn't necessarily isolated to the United States. Furthermore, the simple handshake isn't always so simple. Even in my hometown, there are a variety of convoluted hand clasps you can draw on, depending on your intention.

Urban legend has the handshake originating in medieval Europe as an extension of the right hand, to prove that you weren't concealing a weapon—like a four-foot sabre. Of course, you still could have hid a katara, machete, mace, maul, quarterstaff, morning star, horseman's pick, bardiche or war scythe under your cloak, but that's another story. Europeans were a very trusting lot back then. Since then, the handshake has evolved into a number of different gestures.

If someone extends their hand to me while remaining several feet away (affectionately known as the "Lean-in Handshake"), I usually interpret that as a sign of mistrust—or lousy hygiene practices. It conjures up immediate suspicion and can set a negative tone for the duration of our relationship. The opposite is the hand hug used by campaigning politicians. We've all seen it—right hands firmly clasped, while the left hand smothers the other two. It's meant to instill intimacy and friendship, especially if it's coupled with a gangsta-hug used so often by Denzel Washington when he's welcomed onto the Tonight Show.

Russian men enjoy greeting people with bone crushing handshakes. Anything less is considered effeminate, so if you're attending a convention in Moscow where you'll be meeting a lot of large, adult male strangers, you'd be smart to book a MRI and a consultation with a hand surgeon before you head home. On the other side of the pond, the British use a technique called The Queen's Fingertips—a handshake where only your fingertips come in contact. But nothing beats the Jiveshake for imagination, creativity and dexterity. Associated with young African-American men (with or without gang affiliations), the Jiveshake begins by clutching the base of the other person's thumbs, rotating and gyrating the fingers, knuckles, up, down, inside and out, followed by brushing your elbows, sliding your forearms, jamming your hips and leaning in to bump each others' shoulders.

Next to shaking hands, kissing is the most popular gesture used around the world. It's a standard greeting in France, Great Britain, Arab countries, Belgium, Russia, Albania and Armenia—but not the United States. Even before I'd heard of kissing as a greeting, I'd read about the quaint Eskimo greeting of rubbing noses—called the Eskimo kiss. Unfortunately, Americans are not mature enough to take on the responsibility of public displays of affection—especially in the workplace. A couple of well-intentioned pecks on the cheek and the next thing I know, I'm sitting in the HR department, trying to explain why my hand slid so far below her waist.

The residents of the Polynesian island Tuvalu take kissing one step further by pressing their faces into the other's and inhaling a deep sniff. Personally, I'm glad Americans just shake hands. The thought of kissing or inhaling Herb Mandelbaum's cologne at the start of my annual review is just too much to even contemplate.

There are thousands of other greetings besides shaking hands and kissing. The Japanese are well known for their bowing. The deeper the bow, the greater their respect. It's a wonderful custom and always let's you know exactly where you stand with people. If Soji Kojumora bends 90 degrees at the waist, I know I could probably get away with dating his daughter—or at least asking. If he reduces his greeting to a simple nod of the head, I'm safe in assuming that I'm on his S**T list and should probably look for other friends.

The Masai tribe in Kenya and Tanzania like to greet strangers by either spitting directly on them or into their own palms before extending theirs. And who can top Tibet's 9th century tradition of sticking out their tongues to new acquaintances? It started during the vicious reign of the Tibetan king, Lang Darma who was afflicted with a highly contagious case of Black Tongue disease. I'm not sure what that is, but it sounds pretty serious. Sticking your tongue out at new acquaintances was a safe way to assure them that you didn't have it. Unless, of course, you had just been eating licorice.

People from around the world have always used creative greetings. And depending on the circumstances, you could either make a good impression or instantly bring life long shame and dishonor to your family, simply by how you said hello to a stranger. Imagine the consequences of a clueless German soldier sucker punching Hitler on the arm, spitting on him, high-fiving or giving him a wedgie. Or, some hapless Ugandan Jiveshaking Idi Amin. Perhaps an Italian private sticking his tongue out at Benito Mussolini. Conversely, I doubt my supervisor would appreciate my thrusting an arm out at him and shouting, "Sieg Heil" while clicking together the heels of my jackboots.

In the end, as long as you're staying inside the United States it doesn't really matter how you greet others. Most of our gestures have eroded to grunts, nods or if you're lucky, a text message or a Tweet. Occasionally, a well-meaning co-worker will try to muster up enough energy to squeeze out a "Hello," "Hi," "Howdy," "G'day," "How's it hangin'," "Wazzup," or even a "Yo." If you're lucky, you might even get a nod or a wink. And, if you're a virile young mail clerk or a hot looking chick, you might warrant a slap on the ass.

Become a Breast Surgeon—Online!

As a terminated, over-the-hill computer operator I never dreamed that I'd have an opportunity so late in life to strut down the halls of a major medical center, barking out orders on my way to scrubbing up for a mastopexy.

Going to medical school wasn't even on my radar screen until the sagging economy, a shortage of new physicians and skyrocketing malpractice premiums made it possible for me to reach up and grab the brass ring. And thanks to a deal with the Instituto Tecnológico de Santo Domingo Escuela de Medicina, anyone can earn an advanced degree from the comfort of their living room—even medical school. Using an old 386 Dell PC and a dial-up modem connection to the Instituto, in 12 short weeks I became Allen Smith, M.D.

Getting started was easier than I thought. I spoke with Carmen to determine which of 14 specialties I was interested in exploring: neurosurgery, ophthalmology, gastroenterology, OB/GYN, podiatry, orthopedics, colon and rectal surgery, pathology, radiation oncology, thoracic surgery, anesthesiology, dermatology, plastic surgery or urology. After a few more questions, Carmen took my Visa card number, address and told me I could expect my medical school starter kit in 7 to 10 working days. No college transcript, proof of MCATs or letters of recommendation required. Even the textbooks and lab fees were included in the $79.95 tuition.

As promised, my kit arrived by UPS and contained a lab coat (with my name stenciled over the pocket), stethoscope, sphygmomanometer, a few jars filled with cotton balls, tongue depressors and one of those shiny circular discs you wear over your forehead. Federal law prohibited the school from mailing me hypodermic needles, scalpels and Metzenbaum scissors but they were able to send me a Buckley Retractor, two pairs of Weitlaner-Loktites, a 14.5" Bone Rongeur and a Pederson Vaginal Speculum. My girlfriend informed me that I wouldn't be using the latter on her any time soon, so I had to track down our cat when the time came for my OB/GYN rotation.

After the first week, my cadaver arrived in a 135 lb. FedEx box while I was at the Food Stamp Office. Normally, I'd be concerned about leaving such a valuable commodity unattended in the hallway, but the "Biological Warning. Human Cadaver" stickers on the outside of the box kept my neighbors at bay until I was able to drag it into the living room—soon to become Surgical Suite #1. In the meantime, I had to throw out all of my girlfriend's Jenny Craig meals to make room in the refrigerator for the dismembered torso, arms, legs and head. My first quiz was to see if I could put the six parts together properly.

My second week was the equivalent of the second year of medical school and included anatomy, biochemistry, physiology, histology, pathology, pharmacology and microbiology. I learned how to conduct a comprehensive medical history and a physical and rectal examination on myself. By following the easy to read Spanish instructions on the school's website, I pretended to suffer from Genital Retraction Syndrome and performed a self-colonoscopy. I didn't have a colonoscope, but I was able to build one from an old table lamp in the garage using the provided DVD, "How to Convert Common Household Appliances into Expensive Medical Diagnostic Equipment."

Monkey in a Pink Canoe

The next week, I rotated between neurosurgery, ophthalmology, gastroenterology, OB/GYN, podiatry, orthopedics, pathology, radiation oncology, thoracic surgery, anesthesiology, dermatology and plastic surgery—all online. Each lesson was followed by a grueling 10-item multiple-choice test and a series of coloring book assignments. By the fourth week, I knew I wanted to specialize in breast augmentation, so the school sent me everything I needed to set up a small plastic surgery practice, including half a dozen saline breast implants. There was no way my girlfriend would let me practice on her, so once again, I went looking for the cat. She was still pissed at me from the vaginal examination last week.

To make the surgeries more realistic, the Instituto sent me a Hasbro "Operation" game, complete with 4 DD batteries and a set of CDs that included authentic sounds, like patients shrieking and retching in the background, a nurse screaming in my ear and continuous hospital announcements in Spanish droning over a public address system. They even shipped me an EKG monitor that would occasionally flat line throughout the procedures. To enhance the realism, I emptied jars containing bile, urine, vomit, 3-day-old blood, gastric juice, mucus, sweat and semen on the floor to give my surgical suite the authentic feel and smell of a real operating room.

Every Monday was "Clinic Day." The Instituto sent me an unmarked box with some type of body part ravaged by an unknown disease. It was up to me to examine it, take tissue samples and send biopsies back to the school laboratory with the correct diagnosis. Disorders ranged from simple cases of genital herpes to Blue Skin Disorder, Blasko's lines, Fibrodysplasia Ossificans Progressiva, Exploding Head Syndrome and Aquagenic Urticaria.

Week 9 was the equivalent of the third year of medical school—usually the most grueling. The Instituto took steps to insure that I was sleep deprived with 20-hour work days on top of my usual load of classes. To help me get by, they sent me diet pills, steroids, antidepressants and a selection of black market drugs like cocaine and methamphetamines—the same things traditional medical students use to get through their schooling.

I finally made it to week 12 where I was required to work with real patients. Since I don't drive, the Instituto let me do my final rounds in my apartment building looking for rare, undisclosed diseases in the tenants. I visited Lyman Finwall, Zebidiah Beckermann, Agatha Blaustein and Moses Applebaum. Lyman was missing his nose, Zebidiah suffered from Shingles, Agatha vomited whenever I touched her and Moses thought I was his wife who passed away 20 years ago, so it was just like a real doctor's office.

Achieving my medical degree has turned out to be one of the high points of my life—even though I had to take the final exam 12 times. Had I not been fired from my previous job, I probably would never have embarked on such a big change in careers at 63. Although I see most of my patients in my apartment, I spend one day a month at the VA Hospital in Higbie Corners, Texas. While I don't get to do many breast augmentations on the male World War II veterans, I'm just happy to have a new career. Thank you, Instituto Tecnológico de Santo Domingo Escuela de Medicina!

Employment is a Full-Time Job

I wasn't born to be a sperm donor. Nor was it my lifelong dream to be a gravedigger, dog food tester or phone sex worker—but I've done all four. And worse.

For as long as I can remember I've had trouble settling on a career. Unlike most of my high school classmates who instantly knew they wanted to be politicians, lawyers or proctologists (which I conveniently lump into the same category), my lot in life has been a never ending search for the meaning of life—and where to clock out at the end of the day. Bouncing from one hollow, low-paying experience to another, my job search has taken me to the far corners of the world looking for anything that held the lure of a good income, an opportunity to make significant contributions to humanity, something gratifying and maybe have a little fun.

The first person to identify the secret to happiness in the workplace was the legendary 16th century career counselor, Giustiniano Colafranceso. He proposed the Lavoro Schifoso Triangle—with earning capacity, job description and geographical location making up the Three Legs of Success. True to his theory, a recent Manpower study reported that the happiest people in the world are male prostitutes, Bingo announcers and crop dusters. Colafranceso went on to claim that you can still be reasonably content by satisfying only one or two—provided they outweigh the drawbacks of the others. It's easy to see how the equation works: I was ecstatic working as a hydro colonic therapist making $25,000 a year in Lake Geneva, Switzerland. Certainly happier than I was smelling eggs at Pelican Bay or writing predictions for fortune cookies. I was absolutely miserable as a crematory operator for Walmart, but not as much as a canine masseur.

So, I asked myself, "Why has been finding a rewarding career always been so difficult?" It could have something to do with the Iacobelli Theorem, which states, "For every job, there is an inverse relationship between its potential earnings and the happiness it brings." Sure enough, every time I've followed my parents' advice and taken high paying jobs like venture capitalist, home loan originator or assistant district attorney, the day crawls by with quitting time forever looming somewhere over the horizon. On the other hand, time seems to fly when I'm measuring women's breasts, repossessing corporate jets or tattooing Hells Angels.

Later, I discovered I didn't have to ricochet from one loser job to another like a pistol shot into a rock quarry. There are a number of excellent aptitude tests that can make sense of my career decisions. Tests designed to help me understand what I'd be good at. On my therapist's advice I took a 3-day battery of tests that measured my inductive reasoning, concept organization, structural visualization, numerical reasoning and foresight by assembling dozens of irregular shaped blocks and repeatedly dividing 1,655,783 by 456. At the end of the test, my career counselor eliminated thousands of dead end jobs and gave me the good news: "Congratulations. The tests indicate that you have everything it takes to be a successful state senator, pimp or lifeguard at a nude beach." That was the best $1,000 I ever spent.

Another commonly used tool is the Myers Briggs Test for Personality Types. I'd taken it in my senior year of high school. They claim that before you can settle on the job of your dreams, you need to know what kind of person you are. I plowed through hundreds of questions like, "Which would you rather be: the President of the United States or a bone marrow donor? Which would you rather do: have a vasectomy or watch paint dry?" Somewhere in my responses, lay the clues to my perfect job.

According to Colafranceso, I needed to identify what type of work environments I enjoy most. "Do you like working with people?" If so, I might enjoy sparring with Mike Tyson, embalming murder victims or the exciting world of crash test dummies. On the other hand, "If you enjoy working by yourself, perhaps a plumber on a submarine or fire watch lookout," might be for me.

There are lots of jobs that pay well and don't require a college education. If I knew now, what I didn't know then, I never would have spent four years and $100,000 getting a master's degree from Phoenix University in 17th century Balkan romance languages. Instead, I might have gone straight into auctioneer's school.

Many people ignore what they've learned through organized preparation and fall into the trap of following in their parent's footsteps. For example, succumbing to the pressure of clinging onto the farm that's been in the family for three generations. "Every man before you has been enormously successful. Don't screw it up." No pressure there. Others completely ignore their aptitudes and go into careers their uncles and grandfathers had. It might have led them down the road to domestic violence, debt and alcoholism, but what the heck. They always seemed to have nice speedboats.

For a while, I pondered the old standbys like aerospace engineer, dentist or bomb squad technician. While it's true those careers will probably withstand the turbulence of an unstable economy, I could be missing out on a number of wonderful new opportunities that didn't even exist 10 years ago—sleep therapy, golf ball diving or Feng Shui consulting.

With more and more successful people producing truckloads of disposable income, there's a crying need for people like me to help them spend it. Thousands of customer service positions like phone sex trainers, laughter therapists or feline periodontists provide excellent salaries, benefits and the promise of getting in on the ground floor, while others waste their time slogging through dead-end jobs like teachers, IT directors and nurses.

In the end, there's a chance that none of these approaches will be for me. Even after meticulously navigating through dozens of tests, screenings and bribing my interviewers, there's a possibility that I still might not find my dream job. In that case, I could always do what Giustiniano Colafranceso did when he was first starting out: "Take the first thing that pops up in front of you and try not to piss anyone off." In the meantime, wish me luck with my search! I'm going to need it.

The Boys of Summer

After all these years, it suddenly occurred to me how frivolous I had been. Carrying a loaded weapon is no joke. The worst part of it is no one took the time to teach me how to use it. Unrestricted, I shrugged it off and took it everywhere I went—to the movies, into school, church and catechism classes. I even found a way to hide it inside my Speedos when we went to the beach. Although, to my credit, the only time I brandished it was when I showered or capitulated to curious girls. Even then, I never let anyone touch it. After all, it *was* loaded.

Several years later, as puberty hit full stride, I started reading about how dangerous my weapon was. My cousin shot his girlfriend with his and ended up having to quit school, succumb to a shotgun wedding and take a lousy job in a garage. It ruined his life. I vowed that would never happen to me. I made a pact that I would only bring mine out into the open in the privacy of my room and would never fire it unless I had a good reason—even then, only when my parents weren't home.

Fast forward 50 years, I'm sitting in the waiting room of my urologist, about to have a vasectomy—the equivalent of someone taking away all your bullets, leaving you with just your gun. Oh sure, it would still work. And, I knew I wouldn't harm anyone.

It wasn't a decision I made lightly. Even at my age, I knew that it was still possible to get a young girl in trouble (who wasn't my girlfriend) and destroy all the plans I made, so I decided to bite the bullet and insure there would never be any little Smiths surprising me on Father's Day. I'd take a week of my summer vacation to keep the office rumors down to a minimum and avoid all the taunts when I got back: "Hey, there's my old snip mate," or "Any venom left in the cobra?"

While boning up on the procedure, I read how powerful my weapon really was. A man's penis is to a woman what a .44 Magnum is to a squirrel. Over the course of his life, a man will ejaculate 5,000 times and release 40 to 600 million sperm cells each time he unloads his revolver. Even knowing how bad a shot I was, I didn't like those odds, so it was time to take some evasive action.

"It's a very minor procedure. In 90% of the cases, it takes no more than 15 minutes, is almost pain free and results in complete infertility," said Dr. Cleaver—an ironic name for a urologist. And, what happens to the other 10% of the patients where things didn't go quite as planned?

Dr. Cleaver pointed to a chart framed on his wall with the male anatomy enlarged ten times: "We'll be giving you a mild sedative and injecting a local anesthetic with a needle into the sides of your scrotum here and here. After that, I'll make two incisions with a scalpel directly over your testicles, where you may experience some minor bleeding. Then, I'll insert a hook and pull the vas deferens out of the incision, snip the two little ducts and you'll be through!" After they revived me, I signed the consent form and he left to collect his instruments.

True to form, I fell into the 10% club. Swallowing the valium was easy enough. After all, I was already a drug addict. Having a pretty nurse shave my private parts also helped. Things began to go south when he inserted the needle into my scrotum—"You may feel a slight pinch," he cautioned. Which is like telling Mike Tyson's sparring partner that after the fight, you may experience some minor soreness and discoloration.

After a few minutes, my dreams had come true: I couldn't feel my balls, I was floating on cloud 9 and ready for anything. "OK, Mr. Smith. I've made a small incision in your scrotum and you may feel some slight tugging as I pull on your vas deferens." That was fine. I just didn't know that my ducts were attached to my spine. Every time he tugged on one of the tubes, my head nodded forward. While I had reservations, I told him to keep going. I'd suck it up—at least until we had to repeat it on the other side. Which he did.

The entire procedure took three times longer than promised. I wasn't concerned until he said, "Well, I THINK things went well. I had a LITTLE trouble with your left side, but rather than causing you any more pain and stopping the procedure, I decided just to plow ahead. But there's a chance that we may have to repeat the procedure if it doesn't work the first time." So, I mopped up the perspiration where I had been thrashing about on the table and my girlfriend drove me home.

The post-operative instructions weren't bad. In fact, they made the entire process worthwhile. "I want you to lie on the couch for the next three days and do *nothing*," said Dr. Cleaver. So far, so good. "Put an ice pack on your groin and have your girlfriend bring you all your meals, change your diapers and bring you your pain medication—which you'll take 6 to 8 times a day. When the swelling goes down, I want you to start masturbating like there's no tomorrow. You know, choke the chicken, flog your log, jerk the gherkin, pluck your twanger, polish your knob, punch the clown, rough up the suspect, slap the salami, spank your monkey or wax the dolphin. You won't be completely infertile until you've beat the bishop at least 50 times."

One week after my vasectomy, my girlfriend left me—which turned out to be the most effective form of contraception of all. But, even though she's gone I'm still glad I went through with it. The next time a meet a randy waitress at Hooters, I'll be ready. I'm lean, mean and shooting blanks.

38 Million Minutes to Go

Like most people, I was born with 38,894,400 minutes to do with as I please before I depart this earth and embark on my journey into the next life. If I'm lucky, I'll be reincarnated as a sexier model of my earthly self, with a chance to marry Amy Darowitz, have 10 kids, go to Harvard Law School and become a managing partner at Cohen, Beckermann, Feuchtwanter and Hincklestein. Short of that, I'll just have to make the best of the time I've been given.

Time is such a nebulous concept that I've felt the need to explore it on more than one occasion. The first time was literally the day after I was born. Lying in a bassinet, a diaper filled with digested Similac, time came to a screeching halt. Then I discovered that if I cried loud and hard enough, I could make anyone—including my mother—drop what they were doing and immediately attend to my personal needs. In essence, I had the ability to accelerate time. A few years later, I learned that I could slow time down by bringing home a crappy report card. "Wait until your father gets a load of this," threatened my mother. Anticipating my father's leather belt across my heinie, the afternoon couldn't have moved slower if I was Moses leading the Israelites out of Egypt.

It took me years to discover that I, alone, control the time I spend on earth. If I watch my cholesterol and eat my peas, I could live to be 100. I can add years to my life by having frequent sex, quitting my stressful job, getting more sleep and regularly imbibing alcohol—all of which seem like good ideas, until you consider that I'm not married, unemployed and already spend most my day drunk on the couch.

I can shorten my life if I fly on commercial airlines, talk on my cell phone while driving a motorcycle, hang glide high on crack cocaine, smoke cigarettes and start robbing banks—but not by much. Just by being male, I've already shortened my life by more than 10 years. Nevertheless, I still have roughly 74 years to cram everything into the space that I'll call, My Time on Earth. The secret is to avoid things that make you *think* time is passing quickly, opting instead for activities that make time crawl.

Young children learn this early and attempt to pack as much into a day as humanly possible. That's why you see them running from one place to another, skipping lunch and complaining about being sent to bed. The only time you'll find me running is when someone announces that Dulcolax suppositories have gone on sale. Children spring out of bed in the morning, looking forward to new opportunities, while middle-age adults have already experienced everything that's ahead of them. Sometimes twice. I look forward to discovering that mold hasn't overtaken the casserole in the back of the refrigerator, so I'll have something to eat for dinner, after all.

I started this morning by ignoring the alarm clock. It jolted me out of a deep sleep and informed me that the day had begun, whether I chose to participate or not. I might not have, except for the dentist's appointment I had at 9:00—a great place to suspend time.

Whenever I'm worried about time passing me by, I go to the dentist. Sitting in the waiting room, listening to the patients shrieking and the whine of the hydraulic drill, time stands still. Every time I look up at the clock, it's the same time that it was 10 minutes ago. Suspended animation sets in when Dr. Dentin says, "Just sit tight for a minute. I'm going to go get the biggest hypodermic needle you've ever seen and jam it into your bleeding gums."

After leaving the dentist's office, I endured the afternoon at my mother-in-law's house, listening to her complain about important world affairs: the rising prices of Kaopectate, the new varicose vein she found behind her knee and how broccoli makes her fart. All of this happens with a full bladder because I refuse to use an old person's bathroom.

There are easier ways to slow life down than going to the dentist or spending the afternoon at your mother-in-law's. I worked for a Temp agency one summer when I needed money for mortuary school. Temp agencies have the monopoly on worthless jobs and are happy to thrust you into suspended animation, one assignment at a time. Over the course of four months, I worked as a bank teller, night watchman, meter reader, swing shift call center representative, toll booth operator, Walmart greeter and mail sorter for the IRS. It was like living my life encased in Jello. To help time slip away, I'd come in late and leave early. I'd drink so much coffee that I had to continually use the bathroom. Instead of using the restroom just down the hall, I'd get in my car and drive home.

Finding ways to make time go *faster* is much easier: see how many new apps you can download on your iPhone in an hour, take a nap, followed by another nap, learn how to fly a jet fighter, have sex with your next door neighbor while her husband is outside mowing the lawn, summit Mt. Everest while holding your breath, play the National Anthem using your hand and armpit, learn how to turn your eyelids inside out or figure out how to push a pencil into one nostril and out the other without making yourself bleed.

Once I pass over the threshold into my golden years, I'll be looking for more ways to slow time down. According to experts, the best way to stretch your day is sticking to a routine. Eat the same breakfast. Walk to the mailbox to see if your Social Security check arrived—even though the last one just came yesterday. Take the bus into town to refill your oxygen tank and stock up on Depends. Have lunch at the Walmart lunch counter, then catch the bus back home in time to watch The Price is Right and Jeopardy. It's time for bed.

Regardless of how it feels, my life continues to pass me by at an alarming pace. I can tell because the number of my nightly visits to the restroom is increasing in proportion to the size of my prostrate. That and I just don't have the energy to pole vault anymore. But, that's OK. I'm looking forward to a long happy life with Amy Darowitz and being a partner at Cohen, Beckermann, Feuchtwanter and Hincklestein.

I Remember Hugh

We lost Hugh today. Somehow, he managed to slither out of our second-story bathroom window and was run over by an 18-wheeler carrying a load of chickens headed for a KFC. Considering the amount of time he spent futilely chasing birds, it was a humiliating end to an otherwise, distinguished life. The only thing that could have been worse was if he had been flattened by a truckload of squirrels.

Nevertheless, we'll miss Hugh. But, it *was* his time to go. After all, he was 12-years-old and beginning to show early signs of dementia. From time to time, he'd confuse his water dish with his litter box, so he'd foul his water and walk around the living room with litter crumbs covering his lips.

I bought Hugh for my girlfriend, hoping that he would provide her with companionship while I was away at work. Unfortunately, he took an instant disliking to Natalie and spent the bulk of his days asleep behind the refrigerator licking his balls. That is, when he wasn't spraying the couch or her expensive suede pants.

"We should try something different this time," said Natalie. "Maybe an exotic pet with individuality and charm." Excluding your run of the mill German Shepherds, American shorthair cats and goldfish, I couldn't think of a pet that would be easier on the drapes and didn't need to be taken out in the middle of the night to do their duty. That's when I remembered FlexPetz.

FlexPetz is a company with offices in New York, Los Angeles and London with more planned for San Francisco, Boston, Washington, D.C and Paris, France. They offer a complete line of domestic companions that are available for both short and long term leases. FlexPetz is considered the eHarmony of the pet world and uses a similar, patented Compatibility Matching System that helps identify 39 compatibility dimensions between pets and their owners that are scientific predictors of long-term relationships. I was also drawn to them because of their "try before you buy" program.

I began by registering for the service on their website and made an appointment with Annabel, our FlexPetz trainer, to go over what kinds of pets would best be suited to our lifestyle.

"We just lost Hugh," I said. "This time we think we'd like something in a non-traditional pet that's low maintenance, doesn't mind foraging around the neighborhood to find its own food and does their duty unassisted in the woods. Maybe something that only molts once a year. Do you have anything like that?"

"Oh, I am so excited," said Annabel. "We just received a new shipment of African Pygmy Hedgehogs. They're so cute and love to play with children, although they need lots of room to roam freely at night or they'll exhibit signs of depression, excessive sleeping, anorexia and self-mutilation." I told her I was already familiar with that—I have two teenage daughters. As luck would have it, hedgehogs eat dry cat food, so we wouldn't have to throw out all of Hugh's food—although they do much better with fresh mealworms and crickets. "You can special order them from our African Fresh insect mail order store."

"I don't know, Annabel," I said. "The last time we had hedgehogs, they ruined all of Natalie's expensive lingerie and scared our dinner guests half to death when they crawled inside their shoes. What else do you have?"

"How about something in a nice non-human primate, like a lemur, marmoset or a great ape? They're very affectionate, love to swing from chandeliers and feel comfortable eating right off your table. But, you'll need to get your shots. All of them potentially transmit zoonotic diseases, which means that every member of your family and all of your friends who visit will have to get inoculated against herpesviridae, poxviridae, measles, ebola, rabies, Marburg virus and viral hepatitis, but I'm sure that's all covered under your HMO plan."

"We also have a special this month on Bearded Dragon Lizards from Australia," said Annabel. "They're very independent, enjoy basking on the rocks of the fireplace (as long as you don't have a roaring fire) and love having their spiny scales stroked. Although, they do tend to snag on fine cashmere and alpaca sweaters, so you might want to wear Carharts or other work clothes around the house. Kids love the way they change colors whenever they're upset and about to attack. And, they're easy to feed, too. Just toss out a handful of black soldier fly larvae, wax worms, grasshoppers or cockroaches—whatever you have around."

We continued through the rest of the afternoon, looking for good indicators of compatibility—low maintenance and something that wouldn't scare the bejesus out of us when we got up to use the bathroom in the middle of the night—which, at my age might be 6 or 7 times. At the risk of appearing finicky, we had to start eliminating some of Annabel's choices. We liked the independence of the Caiman crocodiles, but were turned off by their potential to grow 7 feet long and crush our ankles in their jaws.

To appease her, we let Annabel bring in a 13-foot Burmese Ball python she'd been keeping in the back of her trunk for special occasions. We thought "Cleopatra" was cute and really liked the way her black and brown blotches accented the shit stains on the carpet Hugh left behind. The way she slithered around the hardwood floors meant we'd probably never have to dust them again. However, what turned both of us off was Cleopatra's propensity for coiling herself around your neck while watching TV. That meant that one of us would have to be around at all times to pry her free from the other's cyanotic neck and administer CPR.

By midnight, I could tell that Annabel was beginning to run out of ideas. We had already been through hippopotami, Madagascar hissing roaches, llamas, Sugar gliders, Rothschild giraffes and European polecats. Nothing seemed to do it for us. We even thought about trying some unique species of dogs. "If you have lots of cattle or sheep in your condominium park," she said, "You might want to choose a herding dog like a Belgian Tervuren, Pembroke Welsh Corgi or a Bouvier des Flandres." I wanted to try one of the "chick magnet" breeds like a Shih Tzu, Papillon or Yourshire Terrier, but Natalie wouldn't have anything to do with it.

Ultimately, we decided to go with the "Taliban Adventure Pack." It included one mature King Cobra, a Blue-Ringed Octopus, 3 Stonefish, a Blue Dart Frog, half a dozen Death Stalker Scorpions and one Marble Cone Snail—all poisonous. "I think you've made a wonderful choice," said Annabel. They're all so CUTE. And they don't require a lot of maintenance. For the most part, they take care of themselves. Just be on the lookout for their bite symptoms. Things like excruciating pain, fever, coma, swelling, trouble breathing or swallowing, total paralysis—and death. But that almost never happens. You live close to a Level I Trauma Center with a venom specialist, don't you?"

I'll really miss Hugh and know he'll be impossible to replace. Nothing can substitute for the precious way a 12-year-old short-haired cat crawls up into your lap at night and farts in your face. Not even a Burmese Ball python.

You Can't Compete with a Serial Killer

Barbara Tedesco was easily the hottest girl in my Poli Sci class. She was so hot, her aura screamed, "Don't even bother to hit on me until you get your nose fixed, lose those ridiculous glasses and buy a new car." So, when I ran into her several years later, I was surprised she remembered my name, let alone that she took the time to strike up a conversation. I should have known she was up to something.

"How would you like to be a contestant on 'The Dating Game?'" she asked.

After graduation, Barbara took a job as a production assistant with the ABC Television Network in Los Angeles. They produced the popular dating show and sent Barbara out fishing for unsuspecting young bachelors like myself willing to embarrass themselves on national TV. At the time I was a daft 21-year-old ski instructor living in Big Bear Lake—a mountain community two hours outside of L.A.—so I was an easy target for a gorgeous production assistant who promised wealth, women and adventure.

"The Dating Game" was the televised equivalent of Match.com. Produced by Chuck Barris (who went on to popularize other high quality programming like, "The Gong Show," "How's Your Mother-in-law?" and "The Newlywed Game"), it first aired on December 20, 1965 and was televised on and off until the late 1980s. I was abducted by the show during the spring of 1972 and went missing for nearly a month.

When the ski season ended, I left home for my first audition. During my introduction, the producers wanted to find out if a) I was alive, breathing and free from communicable diseases, b) I had any distinguishing features like Elephantitis or a hunchback that might turn off their viewing audience and c) I'd ever raped or killed anyone. Since they needed three available bachelors and bachelorettes every day, five days a week for more than 10 years, it didn't take much to get past the first hurdle.

Barbara was there, so she wedged me into the green room with 50 other guys who looked exactly like me, while we waited our turn to run through a mock-up version of the show. After several hours, they eventually brought three of us onto an empty stage and sat me down in bachelor number two's chair centered in between two other guys. Several director's assistants walked in and started running us through the types of questions we'd likely encounter if selected to appear on the show:

"Bachelor number one, if you were peanut butter, would you be chunky or smooth?"

"Bachelor number two, if you were a peach, would you be the fruit or the pit?"

"Bachelor number three, if I were a Twinkie, what would you fill me with?"

This went on for more than an hour, with one brain-cramping question after another until they eroded our self-esteem to the same level as a stain on the carpet. "Thank you, gentlemen. We'll give you a call if we want you back to tape an episode of the show."

Ashamed and humiliated, I shuffled back to my car as I went over my answers: "Would you be the fruit or the pit?" How in the hell was I supposed to answer a question like that? I would have liked to see how Tom Selleck or Burt Reynolds handled that. As it turns out, both appeared on the show before they became famous—along with Steve Martin, Arnold Schwarzenegger, Michael Jackson, David Cassidy, Robin Gibb and condemned Los Angeles serial killer, Rodney James Alcala. Through some screening faux paux, Alcala managed to slip through the cracks—and won—despite the fact that he had previously been convicted of raping an 8-year-old girl and would go on to murder four women and a child. Sheryl Bradshaw, the unknowing bachelorette who chose Alcala ended up bailing out of their date. Nobody knows why. Either she figured out who he was or didn't care for Magic Mountain.

Several weeks later, I got a call from Barbara congratulating me on making the cut—I was going to be on "The Dating Game."

I spent the next week getting a haircut and borrowing everything I'd need to appear on daytime television. My uncle loaned me his lucky sport coat that he wore to the dog track. I rummaged through the back of my closet and found the slacks I wore to my high school graduation and my dad let me wear his wing tips.

Back in the green room, I met my two co-competitors. Bachelor number one was a bronzed surfer type who looked like George Hamilton. Once again, I was to be bachelor number two. Bachelor number three wore a pocket protector in his short sleeved shirt and had a slide rule hanging from his waistband, so I wasn't particularly concerned about him.

With five minutes to go until taping, a P.A. escorted us onto the stage and showed us to our directors' chairs. Prior to the show, the revolving stage faced backwards, hiding us from the studio audience. Then, the music began.

As Herb Alpert's "Whipped Cream" bellowed from the studio monitors, the stage crept around toward the audience with the lighting heating up the studio to the same temperature as the surface of the sun. As the stage rotated, I slowly evolved from a relaxed, talkative ski instructor into a pillar of salt. Beginning with the tips of my toes, I felt involuntary paralysis ooze upward until it settled into a frozen grin, ear to ear. I was smiling, but I couldn't move my lips.

I don't remember much about the bachelorette—just her questions. She was merciless:

"Bachelor number one, if we were both homeless and living in the same shelter, where would you take me out to show me a good time?" Then it was my turn.

"Bachelor number two, if I came down with projectile diarrhea on our first date, what would you say to me to make me feel better?" I was speechless. Even after a life of creating well-crafted lies, I couldn't come up with a thing except, "Gee, I don't know. I've heard the Kaopectate is pretty good here." Bachelor number three got off easy:

"Bachelor number three, if a group of the Hells Angels hit on me while we were on the dance floor, how would you turn the situation around?" He was stunned. He started to cry and completely dismantled, forcing them to cut to a commercial.

As it turned out, the bachelorette chose bachelor number one. Later, I found out he had won twice before and was on the studio's list of ringers to supplement their sub-standard, mediocre contestants. But, I didn't care. Barbara told me the bachelorette was entering a Tibetan convent at the end of the month and the studio would be sending me a nice Naugahyde briefcase as a consolation prize. I waited for over two years, but never saw it. But, I wasn't disappointed. What's a ski instructor need with a Naugahyde briefcase, anyway?

After I'm Dead

Even though I'm well into mid-life and already straddling the age when men start dropping like flies, I still haven't drawn up a will—living or otherwise. I haven't had "the discussion" with any of my friends or co-workers and none of my relatives will return my phone calls, so if I suddenly meet with my demise, no one will know what do to with all my earthly belongings, money, assets and more importantly, my corpse.

Granted, there's not much to haggle over. The entire list probably wouldn't fill a double-spaced Post-it, but they're all I have and I don't want my TV and water pique going to someone I don't even know at the Salvation Army. So, I thought I'd take this opportunity to spell out my final wishes. All of you survivors can fight over who gets to implement them.

What you end up doing with my body has a lot to do with the way I go. While I'll admit that I haven't exactly treated my body like a temple, my cholesterol is still lower than my I.Q., so there's not much chance that I'll have a heart attack on Superbowl Sunday. On the other hand, I am into a lot of high-risk activities like running with scissors and asking women how much they weigh, so there *is* a good chance that the body you end up with for viewing won't necessarily be completely intact. If I die playing around with my chainsaw, you'll need to borrow an arm, leg or a foot from the mortuary to shove into my funeral suit. If one of my handguns misfired, you might need to fill in the damage to my face with some Spackle, then cover it with a generous layer of Maybelline. All I ask is that the parts match and I retain a modicum of my original ethnicity.

Even though I haven't practiced Catholicism since I graduated from high school, I want a funeral service in a big-ass church—the place where my sister married her 5th husband. You can get the address from her. Most of my friends and co-workers probably won't attend, but since they all said the next time we meet will be over my dead body, there's the potential for a heavy turnout and I want to be able to accommodate them all—sort of like Whitney Houston's service. You just never know how many people I've touched during my life and I want to be ready if they decide to pay their last respects.

I've also taken the liberty of calling CNN to let them know that I'm making my funeral arrangements and even though I have no idea when I'm going to die—assuming it will be sometime within the next 30 years—they should have a team of crack journalists on standby waiting to cover the breaking news. When I go, people are going to want to know about it. There's a chance that Brooke Baldwin, Wolf Blitzer and Anderson Cooper might either be dead or in nursing homes by then, so here's the CNN Headquarters phone number: 404-878-1555. Just tell them you want the Breaking News department to know about my passing and they'll take care of the rest.

The music for the service is also important, so I've taken the liberty of drafting a list of my favorite songs about death that I'd like to be played by my favorite band, The Butthole Surfers: "Don't Fear the Reaper" by Blue Oyster Cult, "After You Die" by Tom Waits, "Don't Need This Body" by John Mellencamp, "Ain't No Grave Gonna Hold This Body Down" by Johnny Cash, "Dead!" by My Chemical Romance and "Done Too Soon" by Neil Diamond. You can throw in a couple of your own if you wish.

I'd like to be entombed in one of those large mausoleums at Forest Lawn, next to George Carlin, Walt Disney, Humphrey Bogart and Michael Jackson. I haven't left any money to pay for it, so you'll have to duke it out with my publisher to get him to cough up the settlement from our lawsuit.

Befitting most Irish Catholics (well, I'm not actually Irish and barely meet the minimal requirements for Catholicism) I'd like my remaining friends and relatives—at least the ones not in prison or rehab—to throw a huge wake in my honor. I'd like the booze to run like a river. Even though I haven't had a drink since the time I drove into Lake Pontchartrain, there's no reason why everyone else shouldn't have a good time. You'll find the guest list underneath my mattress, assuming it wasn't destroyed during the shootout.

Finally, instead of moping around, wearing black for the three months following my passing, I'd like everyone to remember me as a guy who relished life and only cheated the people who deserved it. In that vein, I'd like you to throw a huge party with everyone wearing the costume that they think best represented my life. I might suggest Hitler, a blood-sucking vampire, pimp or a kid wearing a dunce cap. I'm sure you'll think of something. And to celebrate the impact that I've made on each of your lives, I'd like you to wake up every morning, embracing the one character trait you learned from me while I was on earth. Chiseling, self-centered, cheap, fornicating, loathsome, stinky, pathetic and evil immediately come to mind. Or, you can think of one, yourself. After I'm dead, I won't be able to continue doing everything for you.

My attorney has a list of everything I've stolen from you and my fellow in-patients over the course of my life, so see him if you have any lingering resentments and are seeking restitution. You'll have to act fast, though. I've requested that I be buried with as many material possessions as they can cram into my coffin. After I bought my tenth Rolex, my agent reminded me that, "You can't take it with you when you go." As my final gesture on earth, I intend to prove him wrong. Oh, and one more thing. Shut the lights off. I won't be back.

About the Author

Allen Smith is an award-winning writer living in Vail, Colorado. He has been featured on NBC, ABC TV's The View, KYSL Radio 93, The Denver Post, The Funny Times, The Writer Magazine, The Vail Daily and The Tahoe Daily Tribune. His first book, *Ski Instructors Confidential: The Stories Ski Instructors Swap Back at the Lodge*, was published in 2005 and continues to sell around the world. His second book, *Watching Grandma Circle the Drain*, was released in August, 2011. He can be reached at www.snowwriter.com.

Other Books by Allen Smith

Watching Grandma Circle the Drain is a series of laugh-yourself-stupid, read-in-a-sitting stories that look at the way we complicate our lives. Once you read it, you'll never look at life the same way again.

Ski Instructors Confidential is a hilarious collection of stories, taken from professional ski instructors from Alaska to Vermont; from 1942 to the present. Experience for yourself what ski instructors go through during a typical day as they take flatlander novices through their paces in high altitude playgrounds throughout the world.

All of Allen Smith's books are available at

RelentlesslyCreative.com

Relentlessly Creative Books™ offers an exciting new publishing option for authors. Our "middle path publishing™" approach includes many of the advantages of both traditional publishing and self-publishing without the drawbacks. For more information and a complete online catalog of our books, please visit us at RelentlesslyCreative.com.com or write us at books@relentlessly-creative.com.

For readers, join our online **Readers Group** and enjoy free eBooks, sneak previews on new releases, book sales, author interviews, book reviews, reader surveys and online events with Authors. Register at RelentlesslyCreative.com.

www.ingramcontent.com/pod-product-compliance
Lightning Source LLC
Chambersburg PA
CBHW071458040426
42444CB00008B/1392